Utilizing Your Contacts

More Realty Listings

& Sales With People

You Already Know

Utilizing Your Contacts

More Realty Listings & Sales With People You Already Know

Steve Hoffacker

AICP, CAASH, CAPS, CGA, CGP, CMP, CSP, MCSP, MIRM

Utilizing Your Contacts

More Realty Listings & Sales With People You Already Know

© 2013 by HOFFACKER ASSOCIATES LLC
West Palm Beach, Florida, USA
ISBN: 978-0-615-89991-6

———

To list and sell homes, you can wait for interested people to come to you from various sources of marketing and promotion — including the internet and social media — or you can go out and attract potential customers yourself. You can be intentional and take responsibility for producing your own leads by working with people you already know and who know you — and in developing those contacts.

———

Other Sales Content
By Steve Hoffacker

To access or learn about books, eBooks, articles, blogs, commentary, videos, and other content by Steve Hoffacker for Realtors® and other real estate sales professionals, use the sites below.

"Hoffacker Associates" Website
stevehoffacker.com

Steve Hoffacker's Amazon.com Author Page
http://amazon.com/author/stevehoffacker

"Steve Hoffacker's Home Sales Insights" Blog
homesalesinsights.com

"Steve Hoffacker's Sales Quips" Blog
salesquips.com

"Steve Hoffacker's Success Quips" Blog
http://successquips.com

Steve Hoffacker and Hoffacker Associates can be found online at Facebook, Active Rain, Linked-In, Pinterest, Plaxo, YouTube, Twitter, Google+, Tumblr, and many other business, real estate, and social sites.

Table Of Contents

Preface

I appreciate that you bought this book and that you are reading it — particularly because of the importance of this subject.

It demonstrates that you are interested in being an even better, stronger, more productive real estate salesperson or Realtor® than you are right now.

It also shows me that you are willing to take personal responsibility for generating the leads that it will take to sustain you in business.

In many markets, traffic is slower and the number of sales may be less than what has been the case just a few years ago — for both new and existing homes.

Even in more stable market conditions, you might find that you want more contacts and leads than you typically are getting through conventional or traditional means (print advertising, signage, other Realtors®, and your website).

Still, regardless of what type of market conditions you may find yourself in, you can take responsibility for the amount of people that you get to work with.

You can impact the amount of business you have.

You literally can take matters into your own hands.

I like to think of the general theme of what I am presenting to you as "generating customers without advertising."

Typically, homes are sold or listed by having the customer (the interested party) contact you by visiting your office or model home, telephoning you, or contacting your through your website.

Usually they people hear or learn about you or your listings through traditional advertising, such as the newspaper, real estate magazines, or yard signs. They may also see your website or notice a directional sign.

Nevertheless, these are ways of creating interest and attracting customers that your company or broker provides for you, and they can only do so much to bring new customers to your sales center.

Sometimes this is sufficient to make the number of sales that you or your company want you to make. Sometimes it isn't.

Even in good markets, you can supplement the amount of contacts you are receiving and the number of sales and listings you are making by using the concepts and techniques in this book.

However, when sales are slow or you are competing with other Realtors® for a finite number of buyers and sellers, *the techniques in this book can make all the difference in how successful you are.*

I want you to be a self-generator of new business.

I don't want you to feel like you have to rely solely on people that walk through your front door that you had no hand in generating.

I don't want you to be dependent just on the people that traditional or conventional types of advertising and promotion create for you.

In fact, I want you to act as though the only people that you get to work with is that produced from your own efforts.

Treat the interest that is produced for you by your broker or company as a bonus.

If you work with other Realtors® in your office, this will be people that you don't have to share or worry about losing to anyone else — because you will have identified and produced the interest yourself.

I realize that this is probably a major paradigm shift for you, but I want you to act as your entire income is going to come from the people that you produce through your own efforts.

Instead of wondering why you don't have more sales

leads or people interested in working with you, you now can do something about it. You can be in control.

You can do this with no direct cost to your broker or company other than your typical telephone, email, and postage usage.

This text provides strategies and techniques for generating many potential customers for you and your company by working with people you already know or those that are referred to you.

There are specific telephone and in-person scenarios as well as email and letter templates that you can use exactly as they are (or close to it), or you can use them as a guide to develop your own style of contact.

It's time to take an active role in generating more new business and sales, and this text is specifically geared toward helping you develop leads from people that you already know — your existing circle of contacts and sphere of influence.

Utilizing Your Contacts

More Realty Listings & Sales With People You Already Know

1

Why Generate Your Own Leads?

Typical Advertising Is Passive

If you're like most real estate sales professionals and real estate brokers, you don't get to control or influence how most of your customers learn about your homes or contact you.

That's because your advertising and promotion is passive.

While many people will tell you that they learned about you or decided to contact you because they saw a yard or open house sign, most of your new business leads probably comes from some type of print or classified advertising in a newspaper or magazine (such as a real estate publication), a PR story, a billboard or bus bench sign, or information on your website.

Perhaps you have radio or television advertising also.

You may use social media — by itself or in conjunction with your personal or corporate website — to create connections or to promote your listings.

Other brokers or Realtors® may bring interested people to you as well, and people who have worked with you in the past may tell their friends, relatives, and associates about you.

Nevertheless, most customers typically contact you through efforts that you do not directly control other than investing in them and providing for them.

Why Typical Advertising Is Passive

The reason that conventional (sometimes called "traditional") marketing and advertising is passive is because you have no direct interaction with the people you are trying to reach until they decide to contact you.

For a passive message to work — print ad, radio or TV message, online ad, website, direct mail, or anything else that you typically use to get the word out — the person getting the message has to look at it or hear it. Then it has to register with them that they have a need and that this is a possible solution for them. Then, they have to initiate the contact by emailing you, visiting you in your office or at an open house, or calling you.

There's no way to know how many people or which specific people are going to respond to your message until your front door opens, your telephone rings, or you get an email request for information.

Changing The Formula

The issue with passive marketing — regardless of whether you, your broker, or your company places the ads or invests in them — is that the business produced is not always as plentiful or consistent as you might like.

The main drawback is that you are not in control.

There's nothing wrong with sales leads-generated this way. In fact, it's an important source of your new business.

Nevertheless, if you did nothing more than just work with the people who were generated through conventional advertising and promotion, you would not be able to significantly impact your sales output at all.

You would just have to settle for who showed up, when they arrived, and the interest level they expressed.

However, you can be more in control of the amount — and quality — of the people that you get to work with than you are when you just rely on traditional, passively generated leads.

I imagine that newspaper advertising, website visits, or other conventional ways of producing new business aren't enough for you — and that other brokers and Realtors® aren't bringing enough people for you to work with on a consistent basis to sell and market your listings.

How can you make more people materialize?

The answer is by going after them and creating your own following. Take responsibility for producing your leads.

Starting With People Closest To You

Without thinking about it too hard — or getting out a pad and pencil to begin writing down names — there are many people you already know that can begin helping you to grow your business.

The reason most of them haven't so far is because you haven't asked for their help.

You may have relatives living near you, and everyone has neighbors — as well as a circle of contacts, friends and other acquaintances.

Depending on where you went to school and how long ago that was, you might also have several former classmates and alumni friends that you that you maintain contact with or see on a regular basis.

The key in generating and producing new business for yourself is tapping into this network of people that you already know to make sure they know what you're doing currently and that you can use their help.

People Enjoy Helping Each Other

People like to help you when they can. This is a characteristic that all of us have within us.

People enjoy helping each other if they feel that they can and as long as they aren't seriously inconvenienced by doing so.

However, not everyone may be willing or able to help you. That's all right.

Start with the people you know the best and then go from there.

What you are looking for are some people that you already know (even ones that you don't know that well or you haven't spoken to in a while) who might have an interest themselves in working with you to buy or sell a home — or who at least will be able to lead you to other people that they know.

The contacts — through suggestions and introductions — that your friends, relatives, and acquaintances provide for you will include people that you have not met or hadn't thought of who might have an interest in your homes.

The key to this concept is reaching out to people you already know to let them help you.

There is power in reaching out to people that you already know and in requesting their help to generate new leads.

They want to help, and you certainly can use their help. It's a win-win. You can help them — or their friends and contacts — and they can do business with you.

Focusing On People You Know

There are two basic ways to reach out to others for their help in generating leads for your business. One is reaching out to strangers, and I discuss these strategies in a companion book, *"Expanding Your Sphere — Connecting With Strangers For More Realty Listings & Sales."*

The other is working with people you already know. That is the subject of this book.

For the examples and strategies that I present in this book, I'm talking about people that you know well — or at least you have spoken to before who would recognize your name or take your call.

You may decide to call upon family, current or former neighbors, business associates, professional contacts, merchants that you patronize, service providers and suppliers that you use, former classmates from high school or college or real estate school, brokers and other real estate agents from other offices, appraisers, home inspectors, home stagers, lenders, mortgage brokers, sorority or fraternity members, military buddies, social acquaintances, members from the church or civic groups that you belong to, people who have purchased homes from you, friends of your spouse or children that you've met, people to whom you have made a presentation who were not interested at that time, or anyone else that you have met in the past.

Length Of Friendship Doesn't Matter

The length of time that you have known someone is not important.

The period of time that has passed since you last spoke with them or saw them in person is not important either.

The fact that you can call someone by name — because you know them and they know you — is more important than how long you've known them, how well you know them, or long it's been since your last contact with them.

You don't have to be fast friends for this to work.

You might be life-long friends with someone, or you may only know someone that you just met briefly at a social function, seminar, or gathering.

Whether you talk to someone frequently or it was just that one time when you introduced yourselves to each other, people still enjoy helping other people.

People will even help total strangers change a tire, give directions, make up small change at the checkout, phone for assistance, or carry their packages.

If we are willing to do that for people that we don't even know because they need our help and we can supply it, think of how much more people we already know might be willing to help us.

As long as your request seems reasonable to them, people will generally endeavor to help you if they feel they can.

You're Not Risking Your Friendship

Don't worry about imposing on your friendship or making people uneasy that you've approached them. You're not going to be asking people to go out-of-their way or go the extra-mile to help you.

You just want to know if they are aware of anyone — including themselves — who are looking for a new home that might be interested in talking with you about it.

You're not trying to use your friendship with someone to undermine or exploit it.

You simply want to tap into their circle of contacts to expand the number of people you can talk to about your opportunities and services.

As long as you do nothing to jeopardize your relationship, you should not be concerned about the simple act of asking people you already know for their help. After all, you'd do as much for them if they asked.

You May Not Get Any Help Right Now

The people you talk to may not be able to think of anyone to recommend to you, or the one or two people that they do recall may already be working with another Realtor®.

Still, your friends will have tried to help you.

This is not necessarily a one-time request either.

Someone that you approach now may not be able to think of anyone to refer to you at that moment, but they might be able to recommend someone to you the next time you talk with them.

They might even bring it up later on their own as they think of someone.

Raising Their Awareness

If you sincerely believe that you can help people find the home they are looking for or market their current one as good or better than anyone else they might select, you shouldn't hesitate about telling as many people as possible about what you do.

This is why you start with people that you know. You want to help them, and you can use their help.

Approach your friends, relatives, clients, associates, acquaintances, past customers, and others in your circle of contacts.

If nothing more, you are raising their consciousness and awareness so now they are beginning to think of ways to help you.

It's a fairly reasonable request.

You simply are approaching people that you already know and asking for their help — and it's human nature for people to want to try to help if they can.

Whether you are calling someone, emailing or texting them, sending them a letter or card, or seeing them in-person, you simply are asking people if they can help you meet someone that you can talk to about real estate.

There's No Obligation

If one of your friends doesn't want to help you, is not ready to make a move, or isn't able to provide any names for you, that's all right.

Your friendship or relationship doesn't depend on them being able to help you with a referral or by engaging you.

Just keep trying until you get some help.

You're not trying to create any feeling of guilt or obligation — where they feel they have to look at homes with you or give you some names or else you will be disappointed in them.

If people that you already know don't have an interest in buying or selling, that's OK. Maybe they'll be able to lead you to someone else who might.

The more people you involve in helping you search for potential customers, the more successful you will be at identifying them.

Working For Yourself

Be thankful for the people that your marketing generates for you, but be confident in your own abilities to go beyond that and produce your own leads.

If you work in a sales office with other people, you won't have to worry about sharing the leads that you generate for yourself.

You will have produced them, and you can work with them.

Allowing other people that you already know to help you locate and identify people to talk with about your new homes is a great way to supplement the traffic that you get through traditional advertising, signage, and the internet.

You may even get to the point where you will be responsible for the majority of the leads that you get.

In fact, a great attitude or paradigm is to regard all of the leads generated by your company as a bonus and to plan on producing all of your business from own contacts that you generate yourself.

2

Being A Sales Lead Generator

Going Past Regular Advertising

I trust that you are not content just to wait for a new customer to find you through the internet, newspaper ads, direct mail, new home guides, directional signage, or their Realtor®.

There's nothing wrong with this, and it has been the mainstay of sales lead production over the years, but it's just not dependable — and it's not sufficient.

While the majority of your business currently may come from these sources, it is not a long-term strategy for success because your competition has essentially the same access to these resources.

You need to be different — in a strategic way.

It takes initiative and innovation to be successful with lead generation.

Go beyond what your competitors are willing to do and take responsibility for producing your own traffic.

How often are there slack periods or lulls in your business when you wish that more people were contacting you, that they were doing it more consistently, or that you could do something about making the telephone ring more often?

How about having your inbox fill up with qualified email inquiries, or the front door open more often with people qualified and interested in working with you?

Don't Just Accept What You Get

You don't have to accept just what comes your way through conventional sources — from ads (print or web), signage, your website, other Realtors®, or promotions.

You don't have to work just with the people attracted to your office or open house. You can have considerably more than that and be instrumental in producing it.

You can be a catalyst in generating new business and filling those void spots when contacts produced through other, more traditional sources are not as strong or consistent as you would like.

Taking Responsibility For More Traffic

Take it upon yourself to go outside the boundaries of your office or open house to meet and talk to people you already know who might be interesting in selling their current home or moving into another one — or can lead you to other people that you can serve.

This is proactive, intentional contact, and it so often is the missing ingredient in being a totally productive real estate salesperson.

These are advanced lead generation techniques, but anyone can use them.

In the pages of this book that you are now reading are powerful strategies and scenarios for increasing your customer base — all through reaching out to people you already know.

Not everyone who should know about your opportunities may find out about you through traditional means.

However, when you actively take your message outside the office, you can identify and approach additional people.

Rather than relying on the leads that are produced though the efforts of your broker, you now can have a very real stake in the amount of people who visit you.

In fact, I have known salespeople who have created such a following and referral base that they actually have decided not to take any floor time, walk-in, or non-"ask-for" new business.

Of course, if you are in a one-person office, this wouldn't be such a concern — except that you will have created additional business opportunities for yourself.

Nevertheless, the point is that you can create and produce a substantial portion of your business — even as much as all of it — through referrals and proactive self-generation of leads.

Not A Mandatory Action

No one is forcing you to produce your own sales leads, but I imagine that this is important to you since you are reading this book.

Just think of the advantage that you'll have over other real estate salespeople in your marketplace when you become responsible for producing your own leads rather than just relying on customers produced through conventional forms of marketing and traffic generation.

Think of the difference you can make in the advertising budget of you and your company by being a responsible, effective producer of leads and sales without using conventional resources.

Is Self-Generation For You?

Before you get started on your program of generating your own leads to supplement or even replace the traffic that your broker facilitates for you now, it's important to make the commitment to yourself that this is something that you want to do.

Don't undertake it lightly. It is going to require time, effort, dedication, and persistence to do it properly.

If you already are doing so many showings and listing appointments that you really couldn't comfortably meet another customer during your workday, you may not need to generate any more customers on your own — especially if your sales output is at an acceptable level.

However, conditions are subject to change, and in the future you may find that your traffic is less abundant.

If business is slower than you anticipated or less than you would like to have through broker-driven advertising or lead production, you can become a traffic generator to make up for the shortfall.

This is especially true if you are the type of person who likes to have even more traffic than you already have.

Then you definitely should become a sales leads generator.

Lead Generation Is Empowering

Knowing that you have the ability to generate your own leads to supplement what you get — or fail to get — through more traditional means should be very empowering to you.

It can propel you into success while others in your marketplace are struggling or working with the traffic or new business that they customarily get.

Being a sales leads-generator means that you never have to be totally dependent upon your company's advertising or marketing for bringing in enough traffic for you to be successful.

It means that people that you already know — or their friends and relatives that you can meet — may show up in your office or set up an appointment with you for a presentation.

This creates a predisposition for liking what you can show them before you ever begin your presentation, and they are going to like you and enjoy what you have to say because they already are friends of yours — or friends of friends. This is true even if they decide not to purchase.

You have the power to generate your own leads, and this will shape the future of your business.

3

Getting Started

Making The Commitment

The first step in creating additional traffic or leads for yourself is actually making the commitment to begin doing something about the amount and quality of new business that you get.

It's strictly a voluntary program, however. It's willful, intentional, and proactive. It's up to you — and only you — to implement and execute.

It's making the definite decision that you want to go beyond what is produced for you through traditional or conventional advertising, promotions, signage, web pages, and casual or incidental referrals (people that contact you because of a friend or another Realtor®).

Once you make the commitment, you can go about accomplishing it. You can formulate a plan. You can have a strategy.

You have so many resources available to you, and working with people you already know is a great way to build your customer base.

Beginning At The Beginning

The easiest and quickest place to start building leads for yourself is with people you already know — regardless of how well you know them or for how long.

It doesn't even matter how long it's been since you last talked with them.

Begin with the most obvious ones: family, friends and acquaintances, local Realtors® and brokers that you have worked with to show and sell each other's properties, and people whose homes you have listed in the past or have purchased a home through you.

Then you can progress to local professionals, businesses, and people you frequent for goods and services, and friends of friends.

Don't forget to involve your business contacts and acquaintances from church, chambers of commerce, boards of Realtors®, homebuilders associations, Rotary clubs, or other business or civic organizations where you might be a member.

Think beyond the obvious.

Spreading The Word

Don't make any assumptions about your relatives, friends, and acquaintances knowing what you do.

Have you told all of them what you're doing?

Do they realize that you list and sell real estate?

Are they aware of the opportunities that you have?

Are you sure?

Are they willing to lead you to others?

It's time to find out what they know and how willing they are to help you.

Who Do They Know?

When you begin reaching out to your friends, relatives, acquaintances, and circle of contacts with a phone call, email, or personal visit, you are not contacting them to try to get them to immediately purchase a home with you — unless you've heard or they've already mentioned that they are in the market for one, or it comes out in the conversation.

You're looking past that. You want to plant the seeds and make sure they are aware of how they can help you.

The reason you contact them — and nearly everyone else that you contact proactively — is twofold: to make sure they know what you are doing so they can keep that in mind, and to learn about and meet the people that they know who might have a need to work with you.

Then you can contact those people to learn who you can help.

It is not necessary that you know someone particularly well in order to begin a conversation with them about what you do and what you are offering.

Of course, getting a listing or selling a home is your ultimate objective, but you must have people to talk with about your services first.

This is the reason for self-generation of leads, and the reason you begin with your friends.

Just Making The Contact

When you talk with your friends or acquaintances — or the people they introduce you to — you are not trying to make a presentation about using your services or asking anyone to make a decision with you when you initially approach or contact them.

That is likely what you would like to have happen eventually, but initially you just need them to indicate a willingness to help you and then to express an interest in what you are offering, agree to take a look at your homes, or refer someone else to you.

All you are concerned about is making people aware of what you're doing. You want them to be aware of the types of opportunities you represent (not necessarily the specific ones just yet) so that you can create some initial interest and possibly attract people to look at the homes you can show them.

Remember that proactive, intentional contact here means just an introduction to what you're offering — to people that you know well enough to contact but who may not know what you're doing currently.

Since you're contacting people you already know or people that are referred to you by people that you know — regardless of how long it's been since you've actually talked with them — this is not a cold call. You don't need to establish yourself as someone they should talk to at the outset of your contact.

Whether it's a close friend that you just haven't discussed real estate with yet, someone that you haven't spoken with in a long time, or someone you just met briefly at a social event or business function, your proactive contact is meant to let them know what you're doing now and to let them know that you would like their help.

Ways To Make The Contacts

In this book, I provide formats, scripts, and scenarios to use in approaching or re-establishing contact with people you already know — through in-person face-to-face meetings, telephone conversations, and written contact.

You can use them as they are word-for-word, or you can adapt them to your own personal style.

The opportunities for proactive, intentional contact and renewing of acquaintances are extensive.

Think creatively for places and opportunities to contact or reconnect with people that you know and take your message to them.

As I have stressed, look beyond the obvious.

Sometimes you'll want to send an old friend an email or note — possibly a holiday greeting card. Maybe a text message would even work.

Other times you might just want to drop in on someone or invite them to coffee or lunch.

Phone calls are quite versatile and work well when there's a good chance of actually connecting with the people you are trying to call rather than getting their voice mail or going through a receptionist or an assistant. Cellphones are a good place to start rather than the office phone because this is a more personal form of contact.

The point is, there are many ways to contact your family, friends, and acquaintances, and you can intersperse the methods and mix them up.

However, I would only use texting or instant messaging to set up a time to talk, for an appointment for coffee, or as a reminder or follow-up to an earlier conversation.

Your immediate goal is more than just spreading your message. You also want to interact and get some help.

Working Just With People You Know

There are many opportunities for you to meet, contact, and reach out to people that you don't already know or have a relationship with — those you are approaching or meeting for the first time.

I discuss those scenarios and the many opportunities for your success in developing those relationships in my companion book *"Expanding Your Sphere — Connecting With Strangers For More Realty Listings & Sales."*

However, here I am strictly talking about contacting and working with people that you already know or have at least met briefly at a business or social event — anyone that you know well enough to pick up the phone and call and have them recognize your name and take your call.

Begin with your family and closest circle of friends.

It's important that you let them know what you are doing and that you would like to have their help in identifying people who can work with you.

After all, you would do the same for them if they asked and you knew of some way to help them or someone to refer to them.

People Want To Help You

Whether this is a close family member, a distant relative, someone from the club or organization you belong to, someone from your former or current neighborhood, someone you went to school with, a friend or co-worker of your spouse, someone from activities or sports that you do with your kids, someone whose store you shop at, someone you met only long enough to exchange business cards, or anyone else that you know, the point is that you know — or at least have met — each other.

More than that, you know each other well enough for you to walk into their office, pick up the phone and call them, or send them a note or email and have them talk with you.

You know them well enough to be able to ask for their help and not feel awkward about the request.

Remember that people like to help other people when they can — especially people they know.

Don't feel that you need to know someone for a certain period of time before you talk with them about your business — or that people will think less of you because you want to talk business rather than engage in small talk.

Expanding Your Network

To begin generating your own leads, you just need to tell your story to more people than typically walk through your front door or contact you through traditional ways.

That's why you start with your network of friends, relatives, neighbors, acquaintances, shop owners and managers, professionals whose services you use, friends of friends, and anyone else that you know become important — as you ask them for assistance in helping you identify potentially interested people that you haven't met. Then, this will expand your network of people that you know.

Just be careful that you don't expect your proactive contact of people you already know to do more than it is designed to do.

The contact is not designed to make a sale. You won't be making a presentation or asking for a decision.

You just want to identify people in your network to approach and discuss how you can use their help. Then you want to meet others that they know.

This will get you started generating your own leads and free you from total reliance on the people generated by your company's efforts.

It diminishes the reliance on passive marketing and puts you in control.

Four Possible Outcomes

Whether you are meeting and talking with strangers (not the subject of this book but a very important part of your overall lead generation strategy) or interacting with people that you already know, not everyone will have an immediate need for your services.

Some might eventually, but that's only part of the total picture.

When you approach your friends and people you already know and ask for their help, there are four possible outcomes — four things that can result.

First, they can refuse to help you. Don't let this stop

you from talking with them. It's a possibility, but only one of four.

Maybe they think they can't help you, maybe they don't want to get involved. Maybe they just don't want to help even though they know you. That's unfortunate, but shake it off and move on.

Second, they can have an immediate need to move out of their current home and get another one that they will tell you about, and you can engage and work directly with them.

This means that some of your friends and acquaintances become your customers themselves.

Third, they may not have an immediate need to start looking for a new home, but they will want one in the future — and they will share this information with you.

So, you have some friends and acquaintances who will become your future customers.

Fourth, they can introduce you or lead you to other people that they know whom they feel might have an interest in talking and working with you — with either an immediate or future need.

This is the power of reaching out to get help from the network of people you know.

Time To Get Started

Now, with all of this background on how you want to work with your friends, relatives, acquaintances, and others that you know to help you generate new leads that you can talk with about your homes, it's time to actually get started.

That begins on the next page where I present three consecutive chapters of scenarios for you to use in contacting people in-person, by telephone, and in writing (including electronic).

You won't use every approach with each person. Some you may only visit in person. Some you may only call. Some you will more than one approach.

Nevertheless, use these techniques as a starting point and add ones of your own that you like. Feel free to use your own words and style, but this will get you started.

4

Generating New Leads In-Person

Opportunities To Interact With People

There are people around you constantly.

You shop, bike, jog, work-out at the club, run errands, pick up the kids or attend events with them (if you have kids), buy gas, eat lunch, get a coffee, go to the grocery store, get your car serviced, go to the doctor or dentist, talk with your attorney, drop off and pick up your clothes at the cleaners, live in your neighborhood, get your mail and packages, worship, eat dinner out, go places on your day off, go places with your spouse (if you're married), play golf, and go to the pool or beach.

You likely do even more than this in a week's time — considerably more. The point is that people are around you all the time.

It's learning to take advantage of these opportunities when you're around others to develop relationships and get their help in growing your business through the obvious networking possibilities that exist.

In some of your travels, you're going to see people that you already know or who are familiar to you by sight — even if you've never exchanged more than a glance, smile, wave, or "hello."

Sometimes you'll see complete strangers. You may or may not even have eye contact with them.

While this chapter focuses on connecting with people you already know or are familiar with, you will be making introductions to total strangers as well.

These former strangers then become people that you have at least met once — no matter how briefly — and then you can employ some of the contact strategies that I talk about in this book.

Making The Connection

In the next two chapters, I discuss ways for you to use telephone and written communication to reach out, contact, and connect with your network of people you already know and raise their awareness level so they will be in a position to work with you or refer others to you from their circle of contacts.

However, before we get to that, this chapter provides ways just to develop an in-person conversation to generate additional leads for yourself.

Use the scenarios (or ones like them) that I present in this chapter and the next two as a guide to developing relationships and referrals.

The suggested scripts in this chapter will help you as you contact people that you do business with, people you have met socially or at business functions, people that you see occasionally, family members, friends that you see often or rarely, people you have sold homes to or talked with during a presentation, or others that you will have an opportunity to talk with face-to-face about what you are doing and how you can use their help.

Adapting To Your Own Style

You'll discover from reviewing the scenarios and scripts that follow that there are many ways of saying the same thing — depending on your personal style and the degree of formality that might be called for at the time.

You can say *"I wanted to make sure you knew,"* or *"I'm not sure you are aware"* — or you can express a similar meaning by saying that *"I'm not sure if I ever mentioned,"* *"I don't know if I ever mentioned,"* *"In case I never mentioned,"* *"In case you didn't know,"* or *"I don't think I ever told you."*

Of course, you'll know the gender of your friends, but I have used the pronouns *"he," "his,"* or *"him"* for convenience and to avoid using *"he/she/they,"* or *"his/her/their,"* or *"him/her/them."* Obviously, you would use the correct pronouns for the actual situation.

The same is true for people that you would like to have referred to you. They might be a single person or a couple, married or not. In many cases, I have just used the collective pronouns *"they," "their,"* or *"them."* In actual usage, substitute the correct pronouns for the situation.

Visit To Businesses You Patronize

Use this scenario to talk with the owner, manager, proprietor, clerk, or employee you see frequently at a business you visit regularly. Even if you haven't talked much to this person other than exchanging smiles or nods, a friendly "hello," or some small talk, you know each other from your regular association. This would apply to such establishments as a bakery, donut or bagel shop, coffee shop, fast food restaurant, food catering trucks, hotel, gas station, convenience store, home improvement or décor center, gift shop, florist, furniture and accessories store, pharmacy, grocery, entertainment center, arcade, auto dealership, tire shop, boutique, equipment rental, hair salon, quick printer, car wash, bicycle shop, fitness center, auto detailer, post office or postal service store, marina, dry cleaner, tailor, or other businesses in your market that you visit on a regular basis. You want to make sure they are aware of what you do, discuss how they can help you, determine who they know that has an interest in buying a new home — and you'd like to display your business cards or flyers for their patrons.

———

"Hi <use their first name>."

[When you greet them, conduct your regular business, normal interaction, and small talk first. Then begin the following discussion about how you'd like their help.]

"Do you have a minute (Am I interrupting anything, Is this a convenient time)?"

NOW IS NOT A GOOD TIME — [You actually speak to your friend, owner, manager, or proprietor, but they are unable to devote any additional time to you now.] *"I'm sorry I caught you at an inconvenient (busy) time."*

"Have I ever mentioned to you (Do you remember that I said, I'm not sure I ever mentioned) that I sell real estate (represent <name of your company or office — or both>) at <provide the actual location, address, or general description of the area you serve — whatever would make the most sense to your friend>?"

"Well, I'd like your help on something."

"I'll stop back by when you have a couple of minutes (when you have time to talk). When would it be convenient for me to come back?"

[Don't get into a discussion now of what you're looking for — it will keep until your next visit.]

[Wait for response. Agree on a day and time for the return visit if other than your next regular visit to their establishment.]

"Would you like for me to come here, or would you let me buy you a cup of coffee?" [Wait for response about location of meeting — their business or store, or a coffee shop they suggest. Then confirm the location, day, and time.]

"Great. I'll see you <specify the day> at <location>. Thanks."

IS AVAILABLE NOW — [The person you want to speak to has time to talk now.] *"Great. I'll make this quick."*

"Have I ever mentioned to you (Do you remember that I said) that I sell real estate (represent <name of your company or office — or both>) at <provide the actual location, address, or general description of your area – whatever would make the most sense to your friend>?"

"Well, I'd like your help."

"As you know, I've been trading (shopping, eating, drinking coffee) here for <approximate length of time such as a couple of years, 10 years, etc.>, and I thought maybe you could help me."

[Ask them if they have ever heard of your company, but it doesn't matter if they have.]

[Be careful not to deliver a "mini-presentation" even though it might be tempting to do so. You just want to provide a basic description of your services and the area you serve so that you establish a frame of reference.]

"I thought that you might know of or possibly you might have heard of someone (two or three, three or four people) that might be in the market for a different home and that I should talk with them about what it available." [Wait for response — he or she might even say that they are personally interested.]

[If he or she volunteers a name or two, write it down and ask for a way to contact that person or persons. Be sure to note the correct spelling and pronunciation. Get first names so you don't sound like a telemarketer or solicitor when you call them, and get permission to use your friend's name when you contact the other people.]

They Have Names to Give You — *"That's great. I will call them and introduce myself and learn what they are interested in doing."*

"I will call you after I have spoken with them to let you know what happened (how it went)."

"Can you think of anyone else?" [Wait for response.]

"Thanks for your help. See you next time. Good-bye."

No Names to Give You at This Time — *"That's quite all right."*

"I'd like to send you our newsletter on a periodic basis just so you will be aware of what we're offering."

"Is email OK, or should I just drop it off when I come in?" [Wait for the response. Confirm their email address or determine which one to use. You can also send them your contact information or vCard, and send them a link to your website and blog, if you have one.]

"Fine. If anyone does come to mind that you think should talk with me, you can either tell them about me directly or I would be happy to call them and discuss their needs."

"In fact, let me give you some of my business cards so you'll have them available if you're talking to anyone that you think I should meet."

"If you can, let me know who was interested enough to take my card or who you gave one to."

"Would it be OK if I left some of my business cards on your counter or if I came back with a small display?" [Wait for response, and accept the answer either way.]

"Thanks for your help. See you again next time. Goodbye."

Visit To Professionals You Patronize

Use this scenario to visit or talk with the owner, manager, principal, or partner of a professional services firm that you use on a regular basis — either personally or professionally. This would apply to such services as a doctor, dentist, attorney, tax preparer, accountant, ad agency, architect, consultant, appraiser, media people, webmaster, virtual assistant, or others in your market that you or your company maintain a professional relationship with. You want to make sure they are aware of what you do, discuss how they can help you, determine who they know that has an interest in buying a new home — and you'd like to display your business cards or flyers for their patrons.

"Hi <use their first name>." [The person you are asking for might greet you, or there might be a receptionist. Ask for the person you came to see. If they aren't there or available, decide to wait if it will only be a few minutes, or politely say goodbye and return at another time. You don't need to set an appointment or leave

any information. Make sure they know you're a friend or client.]

[When you greet them, give them your current business card, and conduct your regular business, normal interaction, and small talk first. Then begin the following discussion.] *"Do you have a minute (Is this a convenient time)?"*

Now Is Not a Good Time — [You actually speak to the person you are calling on, but they are unable to devote any additional time to you now.] *"I'm sorry I caught you at an inconvenient (busy) time. I realize that I just dropped in without an appointment."*

[They may know what you do. If not, begin here.] *"I'll make this quick. Have I ever mentioned to you (Do you remember that I said) that I sell real estate (represent <name of your company or office — or both>) at <provide the actual location, address, or general description of the area served — whatever would make the most sense to them>?"* [Wait for response, but it doesn't matter whether they remember or not.]

"Well, I'd like your help on something. I'll stop back by when you have a couple of minutes (when you have time to talk). When would it be convenient for me to come back?"

[Don't get into a discussion now of what you're looking

for — it will keep until your next visit. Wait for response. Agree on a day and time for the return visit if other than your next regular visit to their establishment.]

"Would you like for me to come here, or would you let me buy you a cup of coffee?" [Wait for response about location of meeting — their business or store or a coffee shop they suggest. Then confirm the location, day, and time.] *"Great. I'll see you <specify the day> at <location>. Thanks."*

IS AVAILABLE NOW — [The person you came to see has time to talk with you now.] *"Great. I'll make this quick."*

"Have I ever mentioned to you (Do you remember that I said) that I sell real estate (represent <name of your company or office — or both>) at <provide the actual location, address, or general description of your area — whatever would make the most sense to your friend>?"

"Well, I'd like your help. I've been coming here (using your services) for <approximate length of time such as a couple of years, 10 years, etc.>, and I thought maybe you could help me."

[Be careful not to share too much information about what you can show them or provide. You are not trying to deliver a "mini-presentation" even though it might be tempting to do so. You just want to establish a frame of reference.]

"This is where I need your help. I thought that you might know of, or possibly you might have heard of say a couple of (three or four) people that might be in the market for a different home and that they should talk with me about what might be available." [Wait for response — he or she might even say that they are personally interested.]

[If he or she volunteers a name or two, write it down and ask for a way to contact that person or persons. Be sure to note the correct spelling and pronunciation. Get first names so you don't sound like a telemarketer or solicitor when you call them, and get permission to use your friend's name when you contact the other people.]

They Have Names to Give You — *"That's great. I will call them and see what I can do to help. Then, I will call you after I have spoken with them to let you know what happened."*

"Can you think of anyone else?" [Wait for response.]

"Thanks for your help. See you next time. Good-bye."

No Names to Give You at This Time — *"That's quite all right."*

"I'd like to send you our newsletter on a periodic basis just so you will be aware of what we're offering. Is email OK, or should I just drop it off when I come in?"

[Wait for the response. Confirm their email address or determine which one to use. You can also send them your contact information or vCard and send them a link to your website and blog, if you have one.]

"Fine. If anyone does come to mind that you think I should talk with, you can either tell them about me directly, or I would be happy to call them and talk with them."

"In fact, let me give you some of my business cards so you'll have them available if you're talking to anyone that you think I should meet."

"If you can, let me know who was interested enough to take my card or who you gave one to."

"Would it be OK if I left some of my business cards on your counter or if I came back with a small display?" [Wait for response, and accept the answer either way.]

"Thanks for your help. See you again next time. Good-bye."

"Working The Room" With People You Know At A Business Or Social Event

Use this scenario to talk with people you already know when you see them at a social event or business function. This can include parties, receptions, mixers, get-togethers, barbeques, seminars, classes, trade shows, potluck dinners, ice cream socials, homebuilder or Realtor® functions or meetings, and similar meetings and events. After the small talk, seek their help in identifying people to work with you. You are looking for them to provide an introduction for anyone in the room or event that they feel you should meet. Otherwise, this is a prelude to a longer conversation or meeting later.

———

"Hi, <first name of your friend>."

[After you exchange greetings and catch up on what each other has been doing, trade business cards if you don't have current contact information for each other. Give yours out anyway. Talk briefly about what you offer and in what areas. Then, use the conversation to talk about what you want.]

"You know, I could really use your help. I thought maybe you could identify some people — possibly even some who are here — who might be interested in looking for a new home in my area (<name of neighborhood or area>) —- now or in the near future. Possibly some people that you know that I don't."

"Anyone come to mind right now that you have seen here that you think I should meet?" [Wait for response.]

[If yes, ask your friend to introduce you to them. If not, go to the next question.] *"Who (Who else) can you think of that might take my call to let them know about my services?"* [Wait for response.]

[If they volunteer a name or two, write it down and ask for a way to contact that person or persons. Be sure to note the correct spelling and pronunciation. Get first names so you don't sound like a telemarketer or solicitor when you call them, and get permission to use their name when you contact the other people.]

"By the way, let me give you some of my business cards so you'll have them available if you're talking to anyone that you think I should meet. And if you can, let me who you gave one to."

"Also, I'd like to send you our newsletter on a periodic basis just so you will be aware of what we're offering. Is email OK?" [Wait for the response.]

[Confirm their email address or determine which one to use. You can also email them your contact information or vCard and send them a link to your website and blog, if you have one.]

[Discuss and decide on your next contact. You might set a time to get together for breakfast or coffee depending on how close your offices are to each other.]

"I'll talk to (see) you again then. Really great talking to you. Thanks for your help. Goodbye."

An Unexpected Meeting With A Friend

Use this scenario to talk with a friend or acquaintance that you happen to see unexpectedly someplace in public — regardless of how well you know them or how long it's been since you've seen or talked with them. Use this unplanned and impromptu meeting to reestablish and renew your relationship. You want to make sure they know what you're doing now and mention to them that you can use their help in finding people interested in a new home. You may not be able to accomplish all of this in a brief, chance encounter. A subsequent phone call, email, or another meeting might be required.

"Hi, <first name of friend that you meet in public>."

[After you exchange greetings and catch up on what each other has been doing, trade business cards if the contact information has changed. Hand out yours anyway. This may be the extent of what you can accomplish during this brief meeting.]

[If your friend that you are meeting does not have a card, be prepared to write down his or her contact information or have them write it for you on the back of one of your business cards. If you have them write down the information for you, be sure to inspect what they have provided, make sure you can read all of it, and confirm it with them. You know their name, but their preferred phone number and email is what you really need to get.]

JUST A BRIEF CONVERSATION — *"I'd really like to learn more about what you are doing these days and have a chance to tell you about what I'm doing. I could use your help."*

"When would it be convenient for me to call you so we could talk some more?" [Wait for response and agree on a day and time for the call.]

"Great, I'll call you <day and time agreed on>."

"Nice seeing you again. Goodbye."

A LONGER CONVERSATION — *"I'd really like to learn more about your business and what you do."* [Let him or her talk, listen to what they say, and ask questions — pay particular attention to the types of people he or she might know or the clientele served to frame your question for referrals.]

"I could sure use your help."

"I was wondering who you might know that is in the market for a different home that I might talk to?"

"Who comes to mind (Can you think of one or two people) that falls into this category? (Who is the first

person who comes to mind when I ask this question?)" [Wait for a response.]

[If he or she readily volunteers a name or two, write it down and ask for a way to contact that person or persons. Be sure to note the correct spelling and pronunciation. Get first names so you don't sound like a telemarketer or solicitor, and get permission to use your friend's name when you contact the other people they are furnishing. If your company offers an incentive for referrals, discuss this inducement for providing names.]

They Have Names to Give You — *"That's great. I will call them and see how I can help. Then, I will call you after I have spoken with them to let you know what happened."*

"Can you think of anyone else?" [Wait for response.] *"Thanks for your help. Great seeing you again."*

"By the way, if you don't mind, let me give you some of my business cards so you'll have them available if you're talking to anyone that you think I should meet. And if you can, let me who was interested enough to take my card or who you gave one to. Goodbye."

No Names to Give You at This Time — *"That's quite all right."*

"I'd like to keep in touch with you and send you our newsletter on a periodic basis just so you will be

aware of what we're offering. Is email OK?" [Wait for the response. Confirm their email address or determine which one to use. You can also send them your contact information or vCard and send them a link to your website and blog, if you have one.]

"If anyone does come to mind that you think I should talk with about how I can help them, you can have them contact me directly, or you can let me know and I'll be happy to call them."

"In fact, if you don't mind, let me give you some of my business cards so you'll have them available if you're talking to anyone that you think I should meet. And if you can, let me know who was interested enough to take my card or who you gave one to."

"I really appreciate your help. Great seeing you again. Goodbye."

Visit With A Realtor® Friend

Use this scenario to talk with a broker or Realtor® friend of yours when you drop into their office to meet with them or visit them at an open house they are hosting. Use this to renew your relationship — especially if it's been a while since you've seen or talked with them. You want to make sure they know what you're doing now and mention that you can use their help in working each other's listings. You may not be able to accomplish all of this during an unscheduled visit, so a subsequent phone call, email, or meeting might be required.

———

"Hi, <first name of broker or Realtor® friend>."

[Exchange greetings, learn what each other has been doing since you last talked, and trade business cards.]

[Your friend should have a business card, but if they don't, be prepared to write down their contact information on the back of one of your cards. If you have them write the information, be sure to check it, make sure you can read all of it, and confirm it with them.]

JUST A BRIEF CONVERSATION — *"I'd really like to hear more about how you're doing these days and learn how we might be able to help each other."*

"When would be a convenient (good) time for us to have coffee (talk again)?" [Wait for response, determine which they prefer, and agree on the day, time, and location for the call or visit.] *"Great. I'll call (see) you <day and time agreed on>. Nice seeing you again. Goodbye."*

A LONGER CONVERSATION — *"I'd really like to hear more about your business and how you're doing these days. I'd also like to learn how we might work together to help each other."*

[Let him or her talk, listen to what they say, and ask questions about their business and their market experiences — pay particular attention to the types of people he or she might know or the clientele served.]

[Briefly discuss your listings or the types of homes you are working with the most.]

[Determine if there is a possibility of showing or selling each other's listings and then go from there.]

Has a Customer for You — *"That's great. When would it be convenient (When would be a good time) for you to show my listing (address of property) to your client (customer)?"* [Allow your friend to set the time and day for the visit and then agree to it — unless they can't commit to a specific time or you aren't sure of your schedule or when the home can be shown. In that case, agree on a time for you to call them to set an appointment.]

"Great, I'll call (see) you <day and time agreed on>."

"Nice seeing you again. Goodbye."

No Customers for You at This Time — *"That's quite all right."*

"I really appreciate your help."

"Great seeing you again. Goodbye."

Visit With Your Regular Delivery People

Use this scenario to talk with delivery people that you know because you are their customer or on their route — UPS, FedEx, USPS, office supply, bottled water, coffee service, or other messenger, freight, or parcel delivery service that visit your office on a regular basis — to ask for their help. You may not be able to accomplish that much due to their delivery schedules that they have to keep, so an ensuing phone call or email — or waiting until the next visit — might be required.

"Hi, <first name of delivery person that you see on a regular basis>."

[You may not have much time for small talk due to their schedules. If you do fine, but be prepared to get right to your message.]

"I'd like your help on (with) something."

"As you may know (probably know), I sell real estate, and I could use your help in identifying anyone that might be interested in selling their current home or locating another one."

They Have Names to Give You — *"That's great. I will call them and see what they're looking for and how I can help them.."*

"The next time you drop by I'll let you know what happened."

"Can you think of anyone else?" [Wait for response.]

"Thanks. I appreciate your help."

"See you next time. Have a great day."

"By the way, if you don't mind, let me give you some of my business cards so you'll have them available if you're talking to anyone that you think should see what we're building. If you can, let me who you give them to."

"Thanks again. Goodbye."

No Names to Give You at This Time — "That's quite all right. Thanks for trying. Maybe next time."

"If anyone comes to mind that you think should talk with me, you can give them my card, or you can let me know who they are when we talk again."

"In fact, let me give you some of my business cards so you'll have them available — just in case."

"I really appreciate your help. See you again next time.

Have a good one. Goodbye."

Visit With Your Regular
Service & Repair People

Use this scenario to talk with people you know who visit your office, home, or home office regularly to ask for their help during one of their visits to you. This would include your computer technician, copier repair technician, regular phone technician or electrician, the people who take care of your indoor plants, the outside landscapers and yard service, the cleaning crew, and other service or technical people that work with you or your company on a regular basis. You may not be able to accomplish much during a single conversation due to their schedules, so a subsequent phone call or email — or waiting until their next visit — might be required.

———

"Hi, <first name of service or repair person that you see on a regular basis>."

"I'd like your help on (with) something."

"I wondered who you might know or might have heard of in your travels who is in the market for a different home that should talk to me about how I can help them." [Wait for a response.]

[They may need to let you know later or require some time to think about it, but if he or she readily volunteers a name or two now, write it down and ask for a way to contact them. Be sure to note the correct spelling and pronunciation. Get first names so you don't sound like a telemarketer or solicitor, and get permission to use the person's name that is giving you the referrals, when you contact the other people.]

They Have Names to Give You — *"That's great. I will call them and learn what they're interested in. The next time you drop by I'll let you know what happened."*

"Can you think of anyone else?" [Wait for response.]

"Thanks. I appreciate your help. See you next time. Have a great day."

"By the way, if you don't mind, let me give you some of my business cards so you'll have them available if you're talking to anyone that you think should talk with me."

"Thanks again. Goodbye."

No Names to Give You at This Time — *"That's quite all right. Thanks for trying. Maybe another time."*

"If anyone comes to mind that you think I should talk with, you can give them my card, or you can let me know who they are whenever you come in and I'll invite them to come and take a look."

"In fact, let me give you some of my business cards so you'll have them available if you're talking to anyone that you think should talk with me. If you can, let me know who you give them to."

"I really appreciate your help. See you again next time. Have a good one. Goodbye."

Conversation With People At A Special Event Or Trade Show

Use this scenario to talk with someone you already have talked with and gotten to know briefly who has just finished looking at your display during a special event like a kiosk, a trade show, or home expo. Whether they seem to have a specific interest in what you can show them or not, ask for their help to determine if there are others that they can lead you to who should find out how you can help them.

———

[After discussing your listings, answering their questions, conducting your discovery, and engaging in small talk, turn the conversation to this — regardless of whether any additional contact has been set with them.]

"Many people, after they seeing (hearing about) the types of homes I can show them, say, 'Gee, I wish so-and-so could have been here. This would be perfect for them (for what they are looking for),' or 'I wish Fred

and Linda had been here to see this. This is exactly the type of home they're looking for (interested in).'"

[Look to see if they nod agreement or indicate that they have been feeling this sentiment.]

"Who comes to mind that you've been thinking this about as I have been talking with you about these homes?" [Wait for a response.]

[If they volunteer a name or two, write it down and ask for a way to contact that person or persons. Be sure to note the correct spelling and pronunciation. Get first names so you don't sound like a telemarketer or solicitor, and get permission to use the person's name that is giving you the referrals when you contact the other people. If your company offers an incentive for referrals, discuss this inducement for providing names.]

They Have Names to Give You — *"That's great. I will call them and talk with them about what is available for them to see."*

"Can you think of anyone else?" [Wait for response.]

"Thanks for your help. I really appreciate it."

"In fact, if you don't mind, let me give you some of my business cards so you'll have them available if you're talking to anyone that you think is interested in

moving. Just have them mention your name when they contact me or let me know who they are. If you like, you can call (email) me to tell me who to watch for."

[Continue with your presentation, including setting and agreeing on the next contact.]

No Names to Give You at This Time — *"That's quite all right. Thanks for trying."*

"By the way, if anyone comes to mind that you think I should talk with, you can tell me the next time we talk and I'll give them a call."

"In fact, if you don't mind, let me give you some of my business cards so you'll have them available for anyone that you think should talk with me. Just have them mention your name when they contact me or let me know who they are." [Set and agree on the next contact with them.]

Conversation With Interested People After A Showing

Use this scenario to talk with someone who has just finished looking at homes with you and seems to like what they have seen — to ask for their help while they're still with you. You want to determine if there are other people that they can lead you to who should look at homes with you.

[After showing one or more of the available homes and conducting the bulk of your presentation, turn your conversation toward asking for referrals.]

"Many people, after they see the types of homes (what) I have to offer, say, 'Gee, I wish so-and-so could see this. This (Something like this) would be perfect for them (for what they are looking for)' or 'I wish Fred and Linda had been here with us to see this. This is exactly the type of home they're looking for (interested in).'" [Look to see if they nod agreement.]

"Who have you been saying or thinking this about as I have been showing you these homes?" [Wait for a response.]

[If they volunteer a name or two, write it down and ask for a way to contact that person or persons. Be sure to note the correct spelling and pronunciation. Get first names so you don't sound like a telemarketer or solicitor, and get permission to use the person's name that is giving you the referrals when you contact the other people. If your company offers an incentive for referrals, discuss this inducement for providing names.]

They Have Names to Give You — *"That's great. I will call them and discuss what you saw with them The next time we talk, I'll let you know what they had to say and if they seemed to like what we looked at as much as you think they will."*

"Can you think of anyone else?" [Wait for response.]

"Thanks for your help. I really appreciate it."

[Continue with your conversation, including setting and agreeing on the next contact.]

"In fact, if you don't mind, let me give you some of my business cards so you'll have them available if you're talking to anyone that you think should talk with me about finding a new home. Just have them mention your name when they contact me or let me know who they are. Goodbye." [Remind them of your next contact.]

No Names to Give You at This Time — *"That's quite all right. Thanks for trying. Maybe the next time we talk."*

"By the way, if anyone comes to mind that you think I should talk with, please let me know."

[Continue with your conversation, including setting and agreeing on the next contact.]

"In fact, let me give you some of my business cards so you'll have them if you're talking to anyone that you think I can help."

"Just have them mention your name when they contact me or let me know who they are."

"Goodbye." [Remind them of your next contact.]

Conversation With A New Customer

Use this scenario to talk with someone who has purchased a home from you. This can be used at the time of the offer, at acceptance, at the closing table, or even right after move-in. You are looking for people that they know that they haven't already told you about that you can talk to about showing them a home or listing their current one.

———

[After discussing the other issues that you needed to address, turn your conversation toward asking for referrals.]

"Now that you have decided that this home is the place for you to live, I'm wondering who else you have thought of that might be interested in moving as well."

"Who are the first two or three people who come to mind?" [Wait for a response.]

[Be prepared to write down any names they give you (or give them a card that they can use for this purpose) and ask for a way to contact those people they tell you about that they think might interested in looking at your homes. Be sure to note the correct spelling and pronunciation. Get first names so you don't sound like a telemarketer or solicitor. Get permission to use your purchaser's name(s) when you contact the other people.]

They Have Names to Give You — *"That's great."*

"I'll contact them and find out what they're looking for and discuss what might be available for them to see. I'll let you know how it went."

"Can you think of anyone else?" [Wait for response.]

"Thanks for your help. I really appreciate it." [Continue with your conversation.]

"By the way, let me give you some of my business cards so you'll have them available if you're talking to anyone that you think I should talk with. Just have them mention your name when they contact me or let me know who they are."

"Goodbye."

No Names to Give You at This Time — *"That's quite all right.*

"You'll probably think of some later on, and you can tell me about them the next time we talk or even email them to me. Then I'll contact them to see how I can help them."

"By the way, let me give you some of my business cards so you'll have them available if you're talking to anyone that you think I should talk with. Just have them mention your name when they contact me or let me know who they are so I can look out for them."

[Continue with your conversation.] *"Goodbye."*

Conversation With A New Homeowner

Use this scenario to approach and talk with someone that has recently moved into a home you sold them. There's no certain time to wait, but this should be after your initial move-in day visit. You might see them outside washing the car, gardening, walking the dog, getting the mail, watching the kids, playing catch, sitting on their porch, or cutting the grass — or you might make a special visit to their new home. You are interested in their adjustment into their new home and in referring their friends to you.

————

[Greet them and exchange small talk. Compliment them on their landscaping or something else that catches your eye.] *"I hope that things are going well for you in your new home and that you're getting settled."*

[If there are any issues, deal with them as you can. You want them to be happy because this will help with your referrals, but you are not there for housekeeping issues. Keep the conversation away from that if possible.]

"As you're getting settled in your new home and have had people stop by to see it, I'm sure that you have had a chance to think of several people that I should talk with about helping them find a new home or sell their present one."

"Who are the first couple (three or four) of names (friends, people) that come to mind that I should contact and find out how I can help them?" [Wait for a response.]

[If they volunteer a name or two, write it down and ask for a way to contact that person or persons. Be sure to note the correct spelling and pronunciation. Get first names so you don't sound like a telemarketer or solicitor, and get permission to use your new homeowner's name when you contact the other people.]

They Have Names to Give You — *"That's great. I'll contact them, and the next time we talk I'll let you know what happened."*

"Can you think of anyone else?" [Wait for response.] *"Thanks for your help. I really appreciate it."*

"By the way, let me give you some of my business cards so you'll have them available if you're talking to anyone

that you think I should talk with. Just have them mention your name when they contact me or let me know who they are so I'll be sure to look out for them."

[Continue with your conversation.] *"Good luck with your new home, and let me know if I can help out in anyway. Goodbye."*

No Names to Give You at This Time — *"That's quite all right. Thanks for trying."*

"I'm sure you'll probably think of some people later on, and you can tell me who they are the next time we talk. Then, I'll contact them and see how I can help them."

"By the way, let me give you some of my business cards so you'll have them available if you're talking to anyone that you think I should reach out to. Just have them mention your name when they contact me or let me know who they are so I'll be sure to look out for them." [Continue with your conversation.]

"Good luck with your new home, and let me know if I can help out in anyway. I have really enjoyed working with you. Goodbye."

Conversation With An Established Resident

Use this scenario to talk with someone that you have

already met that is a established resident of your market area. You might see them outside washing the car, gardening, trimming the bushes, walking the dog, getting the mail, watching the kids, playing catch, sitting on their porch, doing some exterior maintenance, painting, or cutting the grass — or you might make a special visit to their home to talk about how you can use their help.

———

[Greet them and exchange small talk. Pick out something specific to highlight or compliment them on.]

"As you probably know from news reports and looking around, now is a great time to buy (sell) a home. I'd love to be able to talk to anyone who might be interested in moving. Maybe you've been thinking about this or you have some friends who've actually brought this up in conversation." [Watch or listen for a response.]

[If they indicate an interest for themself, talk with them about their needs and interests and set a time to talk more with them. If not, pursue a referral.]

"Who are the first two or three names that come to mind that you think I should contact about listing their current home or finding another one?" [Wait for a response.]

[Be prepared to write down any names they give you and ask for a way to contact those people. Be sure to note the correct spelling and pronunciation. Get first names so you don't sound like a telemarketer or solicitor. Get permission to use the name of the person giving you the referrals when you contact the other people.]

They Have Names to Give You — *"That's great. I'll contact them and see how I can help them, and the next time we talk I'll let you know what happened."*

"Can you think of anyone else?" [Wait for response.]

"Thanks for your help. I really appreciate it."

"By the way, let me give you some of my business cards so you'll have them available if you're talking to anyone that you think should talk with me. Just have them mention your name when they contact me or let me know who they are so I'll be sure to look out for them."

"I really appreciate the confidence you have shown in me and your willingness to help. It means a lot to me."

"Goodbye. Have a great day."

No Names to Give You at This Time — *"That's quite all right. Thanks for trying. Maybe another time."*

"I'm sure you'll think of some people later on, and you can tell me who they are the next time we talk or you

can get hold of me by phone or email. Then I'll contact them and see how I can help them."

"By the way, let me give you some of my business cards so you'll have them available if you're talking to anyone that you think I should talk with. Just have them mention your name when they contact me or let me know who they are so I'll be sure to look out for them."

"Goodbye and have a great day."

Conversation With A Referring Resident

Use this scenario to talk with someone that has been a resident of your market area that you already have met and who has furnished you with leads in the past — to thank them and request their help again.

———

[Greet them and exchange small talk. Pick out something specific to compliment them on or highlight.]

"I really value your trust and confidence that you have shown in me by telling other people about my services and allowing me to contact them. It means a lot to me, but I still can use your assistance."

"We all meet new people all the time — or think of

ones that we hadn't thought of before — so in addition to your friends (former neighbors, relatives, co-workers, associates, colleagues, clients) that you've already told me about, I thought I'd check with you to see which two or three people you might have met recently or that you hadn't thought about before that you think I should with about their plans for moving or finding another home." [Wait for response.]

[Be prepared to write down any names they give you and ask for a way to contact those people. Be sure to note the correct spelling and pronunciation. Get first names so you don't sound like a telemarketer or solicitor. Get permission to use your referring resident's name when you contact the other people.]

They Have Names to Give You — "That's great. I'll contact them like I did the others you told me about and see how I can help them. The next time we talk I'll let you know what happened."

"Can you think of anyone else?" [Wait for response.]

"Thanks for your help. I really appreciate it."

"By the way, let me give you some more of my business cards so you'll have them available if you're talking to anyone that you think I should contact. Just let me know who they are so I'll be sure to look out for them. If you like, you can call or email to tell me who to watch for."

"Goodbye and have a great day."

No Names to Give You at This Time — *"That's quite all right. Thanks for trying. Maybe the next time."*

"I'm sure you'll probably think of some more people later on, and you can tell me who they are the next time we talk or you can email me or give me a call."

"Then I'll contact them like I did before and see how I can help them."

"By the way, let me give you some more of my business cards so you'll have them available if you're talking to anyone that you think I should speak with. Just let me know who they are so I'll be sure to look out for them. If you like, you can call or email to tell me who to watch for."

"Goodbye and have a great day."

5

Connecting By Telephone

The Value Of Telephone Contact

Planned, or even impromptu, in-person meetings and conversations are great for interacting and connecting with friends and acquaintances.

Smiles, shrugs, hand gestures, grins, chuckles, laughs, raised eyebrows, a touch, rolling of the eyes, surprised or shocked looks, anger, disgust, frustration, elation, frowns, confusion, empathy, and other expressions of emotion are immediately conveyed during a face-to-face meeting or conversation.

However, that type of contact — as ideal as it is — isn't always necessary, available, or convenient. The person you want to talk with could be hundreds or even thousands of miles away.

Therefore, the next best thing to talking to someone in-person is speaking to them by phone.

The telephone is a powerful way of reaching out and staying connected with your circle of contacts.

While you can't see what each other is saying and how you are communicating your message (unless you're using webcams, FaceTime, or Skype), you still get to hear each other and often can sense how the other is speaking — particularly if you know them fairly well.

Your "Circle Of Contacts"

All of us know people from a variety of sources — family, school, former employers and employees, colleagues, customers, current and former neighborhoods, church, clubs, organizations, community and civic groups, recreational activities, charities, local businesses and professionals, and friends of our kids and spouse.

Many people refer to this network of friends, family, and associates that we have as our "sphere of influence," but I don't think this is a great term to use.

Rather, I use a more inclusive term that applies to all the people we know — regardless of how we met them, how well we might know them, how long we have known them, and when we last spoke to them.

I simply call it our "circle of contacts."

Undoubtedly, you have a database of your contacts stored as a stack of business cards in your rolodex or in a drawer, a more formal arrangement of them in your computer in a CRM (contact/customer relational manager) such as ACT! or Outlook, in your PDA, on your smartphone, or on more than one of these.

Anytime you want, you can pick up the telephone and reach out to any of your of contacts. You probably even have the numbers of the people you call the most memorized or on speed dial.

The nice thing about using the phone to contact people is that you don't have to get in your car or leave your home or office. No special preparation is required other than what you want to say and who you want to call.

You Know Many People

In addition to your family, neighbors, close friends, colleagues, associates, and others you see or socialize with on a regular basis, there are many other business contacts that you can rely upon to help you generate leads and build your business.

These include other salespeople in your market that you have a good relationship with that offer a variety of goods and services — whether you do business with

them or just know them, other brokers and Realtors®
that you know, professional contacts such as attorneys
and physicians that you know in your market area, and
businesses that you patronize regularly.

You also have names and phone numbers for appraisers,
home inspectors, interior decorators, home stagers,
remodelers, contractors, painters, electricians, pool
service, landscapers, movers, entertainment and
recreational facilities you use, governmental offices,
and similar places where you know people.

Add to that the customers you've sold homes to or for
and the ones you're still working with to help them find
their perfect home.

Your data bank is full of names and phone numbers.

Getting Started

All you need to do is begin tapping into this major
resource as you reach out and connect with people you
already know and ask for their help.

You need business and you want referrals. They can
help you, and they want to help you. You just need to
ask and make them aware of what you need.

We already addressed calling on people in-person or
seeing them in public. This chapter focuses specifically

on using the telephone to connect with people that you already know in some way.

I'm talking about telephoning people that you already know well enough — even if you haven't seen or spoken with them in a while — to be able to pick up the phone, call them, and have them take your call and speak with you.

There's nothing to be apprehensive about.

You're calling your friends, other people who know you, or those who recognize your name well enough to take your call and speak with you.

Not everyone may agree to help or feel that they are capable of helping you, but your request is legitimate and is not based on testing or taking advantage of your friendship.

Tapping Into A Willingness

In this chapter, I give you some suggested language to use for your telephone conversations as you reach out to people that can help you. Use it as it is or as a guide.

Just remember that the people you are calling are not strangers. Some you will know better than others, and some longer than others. However, there is no reason not to call them and ask for their help.

People like to help you if they know what you need and feel that it's something they can do.

It's human nature to want to help someone if we feel that we can and that we won't be too inconvenienced by doing so.

You just need to ask the people you're calling for their help and make them aware of what you need. Then reassure them that they have the ability to help you.

Call After A Brief Introduction

Use this scenario for your telephone call the day after or soon after meeting someone initially and talking briefly with them at a business or social function or in public. Primarily you want to talk with them some more or set up a meeting with them to determine if they have an interest in what you can offer them and who they might know that has an interest in moving or buying a home.

———

"Hello <use their first name>? This is <your name> from <name of your company>."

"I met you <last night, Tuesday, yesterday, the other day, last week, or recently> at the <mention the specific event or place where you met, such as Chamber of Commerce breakfast, church, Little

League game, the mall, a specific store or restaurant, the Rotary Club, etc.> and we met just long enough to exchange business cards and that was about it."

"Do you have a quick minute now or should I call back?" [Wait for response.]

NOW IS NOT A GOOD TIME — [You actually speak to your new friend or acquaintance, but they are unable to devote any additional time to you now.] "No problem. Let me call back when you have a minute."

"I just wanted to call to say hello again and to set a convenient (good) time when I could stop by to meet with you for a few minutes." [Set up a convenient time to talk again, but do not set the appointment to meet at this time unless they insist and will talk long enough to set the future appointment but no more.] "Goodbye."

HAS JUST A QUICK MINUTE NOW — [You actually get to speak to the person you are calling, but they don't have much time to talk — just set an appointment for the next contact.] "Great. I'll make this quick."

"I just wanted to call to say hello again and to set a convenient (good) time when I could stop by for a couple of minutes or grab a cup of coffee to learn a little bit more about your business (what you do) and let you know what I am looking for."

"Which one is better for you <meeting at their office or a coffee shop>?" [Wait for response.]

"Fine." [Agree on the place, date, and time]

"I look forward to seeing you again then on <date of the appointment> at <agreed time> at <agreed location>."

"Would you like for me to email you a reminder?" [Wait for response.]

> **Yes** — *"Fine. I'll send you a note on <specific day> to remind you of our appointment on <day, time, and location>. Which email address should I use?"* [Confirm the address or write it down as you obtain it.]
>
> *"I look forward to seeing (meeting) you again then. Goodbye."*
>
> **No** — *"Fine. I'll plan on seeing you then on <mention the day and time> at <place>. Goodbye."*

Call To A Social Networking Contact

Use this scenario to call any person that you know through social networking sites because you have commented on their site or officially connected with them so that they know who you are. You mainly want to talk with them — rather than set a meeting — to determine who they know in your area who has an interest in buying a new home and who they can refer to you. Call them on their cell phone to avoid office voice mail and "screeners." They could be across town or miles away from your location.

———

"Hello <use their first name>? This is <your name>."

"I know you from <name of networking site where you both are a member>. [The person you are calling should immediately recognize your name.]

"Do you have a quick minute?" [Wait for response.]

NOW IS NOT A GOOD TIME — *"No problem. I know you weren't expecting my call right now. Let me call back when you have a minute."* [Set up a convenient time to talk again.]

"I'll give you a call again on <date agreed, and possibly set a specific time as well>. Goodbye."

IS AVAILABLE NOW — *"Great. I'll make this fairly quick."*

"As you may (probably) know, I sell real estate in <name of your area or town>. I thought maybe you could help me identify people who might be interested in looking for a new home in my area — now or in the near future."

[Listen for their general willingness to help you. If he

or she mentions that they would like to help, set up another call at a mutually convenient time. If they volunteer a name or two, write it down and ask for a way to contact that person or persons. Be sure to note the correct spelling and pronunciation. Get first names so you don't sound like a telemarketer or solicitor when you call them, and get permission to use their name when you contact the other people. If there seems to be no interest in helping you or in establishing a professional relationship, conclude the call.]

"Good speaking with you. Thanks for taking my call. See you online. Goodbye."

Call To A Friend Or Acquaintance

Use this scenario to call and talk with someone you know very well — or well enough to speak to each other and have a conversation when you meet. You want to make sure they know what you are doing and that you want to enlist their help in identifying people that they know that might be interested in selling their present home or looking for another one.

_____

"Hi, <first name or nickname of your friend>. This is <your name — possibly just your first name>."

"I wasn't sure if you were aware (I'm not sure whether you heard/know) that I am (began) working with <name

of your company> (started my own real estate business). I just started (I've been doing this a few weeks (months)."

"I'd really like to catch up with you and learn more about what you're doing and get a chance to talk you about my direction and what's going on right now. Also, I could use your help."

"Do you have a few minutes now or would it be better for me to call back at another time?" [Wait for response.]

Now Is OK — "*Fine.*" [Discuss what your friend is doing. You also can set a time to get together for breakfast or coffee depending on how close your offices are to each other. Then talk about what you are doing and what you need. Listen for an indication of interest.]

"I mentioned that I can use your help. I thought maybe you could help me identify people who might be interested in looking for a new home in my area — now or in the near future. Possibly some people that you know that I don't. Maybe even you."

"Who are the first couple of names that come to mind right now that you think would take my call so I could find out about what they might be looking for and how I could help them?" [Wait for response.]

[If they volunteer a name or two, write it down and ask for a way to contact that person or persons. Be sure to note the correct spelling and pronunciation. Get first names so you don't sound like a telemarketer or solicitor when you call them, and get permission to use their name when you contact the other people.]

"I'd like to send you our newsletter on a periodic basis just so you will be aware of what the real estate market is doing. Is email OK?" [Wait for the response. Confirm their email address or determine which one to use. You can also send them your contact information or vCard and send them a link to your website and blog, if you have one. Then, discuss your next contact and agree on when and where that is to be and if it's by email, phone, or in-person.]

"I'll talk to (see) you again then. Really great talking to you. Thanks for your time. Goodbye."

NOW IS NOT A GOOD TIME — *"I knew that you might be busy and that you weren't expecting my call right now, but I thought I'd take a chance."*

"Let me call back when you have a minute." [Set up a convenient time to talk again.] *"Talk to you then. Goodbye."*

Call From A Friend Or Acquaintance

Use this scenario to talk with someone you know very well or well enough to have a conversation — when they call you for whatever reason. They will be calling you on your cell phone since the presumption is that they don't know where you are working. You might recognize their phone number or their voice. You want to make sure they know what you are doing now, where you're doing it, and that you want to enlist their help in identifying people that they know that might be interested in moving into another home.

———

[Answer the phone. Hear the other person identify themself.] *"Hi, <first name or nickname of your friend>."*

[Listen to them and discuss what they want to talk about with you. Then at an appropriate moment, change gears and use the conversation to talk about what you want.]

"I recently began selling real estate with <name of your company> (opened my own real estate office) and we're located at/in <a general description is probably enough>."

"You know, I could really use your help. Do you have another minute now or would it be better for me to give you a call back later?" [Wait for response.]

Now Is OK — *"Fine. I thought maybe you could help me identify some people who might be interested in looking for a new home in my area — now or in the near future. Possibly some people that you know that I don't. Maybe even you."*

"Who are the first couple of names that come to mind right now that you think would take my call to talk about what they're looking for and how I might help them?" [Wait for response.]

[If they volunteer a name or two, write it down and ask for a way to contact that person or persons. Be sure to note the correct spelling and pronunciation. Get first names so you don't sound like a telemarketer or solicitor when you call them, and get permission to use their name when you contact the other people.]

"I'd like to send you our newsletter on a periodic basis just so you will be aware of what the real estate market is doing. Is email OK?" [Wait for the response. Confirm their email address or determine which one to use. You can also send them your contact information or vCard and send them a link to your website and blog, if you have one.]

[Discuss your next contact and agree on when and where that is to be and if it's by email, phone, or in-person. You might set a time to get together for breakfast or coffee depending on how close your offices are to each other.]

"I'll talk to (see) you again then (at that time)."

"Really great talking to you again. Thanks for the call and for your help. Goodbye."

LATER WOULD BE BETTER — *"That's fine. It can wait."* [Set up a convenient time to talk again.] *"Talk to you then. Goodbye."*

Call To An Old Contact

Use this scenario to call and talk with someone you know from your past well enough to speak to each other — but it's been a long time since you saw or spoke to each other. You want to make sure they know what you are doing currently and that you want to enlist their help in identifying people that they know that might be interested in moving or looking at or purchasing a new home that you can show them.

—————

"Hi, <first name or nickname of your friend>, this is <your name>."

"How have you been? It's been a long time." [Wait for response.]

"We haven't talked in a while so I wanted to make sure that you knew that I am (began) selling real estate with <name of your company> (opened my own real estate office) and we're located at <a general description is probably enough>."

"I wanted to say hello and make sure you are doing well since it's been a while (long time) since we talked, but

the main reason for my call is that I'd like for you to know what I'm doing, and that I could use your help. Do you have a moment now or would it be better for me to call back at a better time?" [Wait for response.]

Now Is OK — *"Fine. I thought maybe you could help me identify people who might be interested in looking for a new home in my area — now or in the near future. Possibly some people that you know that I don't — maybe even yourself* [if they live near where you are selling]. *"*

"Who are the first couple of names that come to mind right now that you think would take my call to discuss how I can help them?" [Wait for response.]

[If they volunteer a name or two, write it down and ask for a way to contact that person or persons. Be sure to note the correct spelling and pronunciation. Get first names so you don't sound like a telemarketer or solicitor when you call them, and get permission to use their name when you contact the other people.]

"I'd like to send you our newsletter on a periodic basis just so you will be aware of what is going on in the area. Is email OK?" [Wait for the response. Confirm their email address or determine which one to use. You can also send them your contact information or vCard and send them a link to your website and blog, if you have one.]

[Discuss your next contact and agree on when and

where that is to be and if it's by email, phone, or in-person. You can set a time to re-establish your relationship by getting together for coffee depending on how close your offices are to each other.]

"I'll talk to (see) you then. Really great talking to you again. Thanks for your help. Goodbye."

NOW IS NOT A GOOD TIME — *"I knew that you might be busy and that you weren't expecting my call right now, but I thought I'd take a chance. Let me call back when you have a minute."* [Set up a convenient time to talk again.] *"Talk to you then. Goodbye."*

Call From An Old Contact

Use this scenario when you get an unexpected call from someone from your past that you know somewhat well — but it's been a long time since you spoke or saw each other. During this call, you want to make sure they know what you are doing now and that you want to enlist their help in identifying people that they know that might be interested in selling their current home or purchasing a new home with you.

———

[Answer the phone. Hear the other person identify themself.] *"Hi, <first name or nickname of your friend>. Boy, it's been a while. Great to hear from you."*

[Listen to them and discuss what they want to talk with you about since they called you. Then at an appropriate moment, change gears and use the conversation to talk about what you are doing now and how you want their help.]

"*I'm now working (selling real estate) with <name of your company> (I opened my own real estate office) and we're located at <a general description is probably enough>.*" [Talk very briefly about the homes you focus on — size, price range, general area, and market segment.]

"*You know, I could really use your help. Do you have another minute now or would it be better for me to give you a call later?*" [Wait for response.]

Now Is OK — "*Fine. I thought maybe you could help me identify some people — maybe even you — who might be interested in looking for a new home in my area — now or in the near future. Possibly some people that you know that I don't.*"

"*Who are the first couple of names that come to mind right now that you think would take my call to let them know how I can help them?*" [Wait for response.]

[If they volunteer a name or two, write it down and ask for a way to contact that person or persons. Be sure to note the correct spelling and pronunciation. Get first names so you don't sound like a telemarketer or solicitor when you call them, and get permission to use their name when you contact the other people.]

"I'd like to send you our newsletter on a periodic basis just so you will be aware of what's going on in local real estate [if they are living in your area]. *Is email OK?"* [Wait for the response. Confirm their email address or determine which one to use. You can also send them your contact information or vCard and send them a link to your website and blog, if you have one.]

[Discuss your next contact and agree on when and where that is to be and if it's by email, phone, or in-person. You might set a time to get together for coffee depending on how close your offices are to each other.]

"I'll talk to (see) you again then. Really great hearing from you. Thanks for the call and your help. Goodbye."

LATER WOULD BE BETTER — *"That's fine. It can wait."* [Set up a convenient time to talk again.] *"Talk to you then. Goodbye."*

Call To A Realtor® Friend

Use this scenario to call and talk with a fellow Realtor® from another office that you know very well or at least professionally. You could have met them before you got into real estate sales. You want to make sure they know what you're doing now and that you can help each other with sales.

———

"Hi, <first name or nickname of your Realtor® friend>."

"I wanted to make sure that you're aware that I recently began working (selling real estate) with <name of your company> (opened my own real estate office) and we're located at <a general description is probably enough>. So now we're colleagues."

"You know, I think we could help each other. Do you have another minute now or would it be better for me to give you a call later?" [Wait for response.]

Now Is OK — *"Fine. Are you working with anyone (Who are you working with) that you could bring by to look at my listings (open houses)?"* [Wait for response and be prepared to talk a little about the nature of your listings or open houses.]

Has a Customer for You — *"That's great. When would it be convenient (When would be a good time) for you to visit with your customer(s)?"*

[Set and agree on the time for the visit unless they need check with their customer first — agree on a time to call them to set an appointment.]

"Great, I'll call you <day and time agreed on> (see you <day and time agreed on> at <location of home for sale>). Do you need directions?" [Wait for response and provide directions if needed or agree to email or fax a map — obtain or confirm email address or the fax number to use.] *"Nice talking with you again. Goodbye."*

No Customers for You at This Time — *"That's quite all right. Maybe we can work together in the future."*

"By the way, what do you have that I can help you sell?" [Wait for the response.]

LATER WOULD BE BETTER — *"That's fine. It can wait."* [Set up a convenient time to talk again.] *"Talk to you then. Goodbye."*

Call To A New Customer

Use this scenario to call and talk with someone who has purchased a new home through your efforts — or listed one with you. This can be used anytime after the initial listing appointment or after the offer has been made but *before* closing on the existing home sale or purchase of the new one. You want to help keep them excited about their decision to work with you and request their help in identifying people that they know that you can contact about working with you to market their homes or look at homes you can show them.

———

"Hi, <first name or nickname of your customer>."

[Thank them again for their purchase or agreeing to list their current home with you, complete your small talk, and then get to the reason for your call.]

"You've probably had a chance to think of a few (a couple, several) of your friends or associates that you feel should meet with me to discuss putting their home on the market or to begin looking for one that will meet their needs better than their current one." [Wait for response.]

"Who are the first couple of (two or three, few) people who come to mind that you think really ought to talk with me?" [Wait for a response and be prepared to write down any names they give you and ask for a way to contact the friends that they tell you about. Be sure to note the correct spelling and pronunciation. Get first names so you don't sound like a telemarketer or solicitor. Get permission to use your customer's name when you contact the other people.]

They Have Names to Give You — *"That's great. I'll contact them and see I how I can help them, and I'll let you know what happened. Can you think of anyone else?"* [Wait for response.]

"Thanks for your help. I really appreciate it. Please let me know if there's anything I can do for you. Goodbye."

No Names to Give You at This Time — *"That's quite all right. You'll probably think of some later on, and you can tell me about them the next time we talk or you can email them to me. Then I'll contact them and see how I can help them. Please let me know if there's anything I can do for you. Goodbye."*

Call To Existing Residents

Use this scenario to call and talk with residents of your market or farm area that you have met and know personally. Even if they have lived in their home for several years or you have not worked with them previously, you have spoken to them in the past and developed a relationship with them. You want to know if they might be thinking of moving or who they know that might have a need for your services.

———

"Hi, <first name or nickname of resident>." [Complete your small talk, and then get to the reason for your call.]

"We've talked before about real estate, and I wanted to see if you had any interest in moving or finding a different home at this time?" [Wait for response.]

[If they express some interest in talking or meeting with you, set an appointment for later rather than trying to get into too many details on this unscheduled phone call. If they have no interest, ask them for referrals.]

"I'd like your help for a minute. I imagine you've probably thought of (heard about) some of your friends or associates that you think might be interested in moving that I should speak with about how I might be able to help them." [Wait for response.]

"Who are the first couple of (two or three) people who come to mind that you think I ought to talk with?" [Wait for a response. Be prepared to write down any names they give you and ask for a way to contact them. Be sure to note the correct spelling and pronunciation. Get first names so you don't sound like a telemarketer or solicitor. Get permission to use your resident's name when you contact the other people.]

They Have Names to Give You — *"That's great. I'll contact them and see how I can help them, and I'll let you know what happened. Can you think of anyone else?"* [Wait for response.]

"Thanks for your help. I really appreciate it. Please let me know if there's anything I can do for you. Goodbye."

No Names to Give You at This Time — *"That's quite all right. You'll probably think of some people later on, and you can tell me about them the next time we talk or you can email them to me. Then I'll contact them to see how I can be of assistance to them. Please let me know if there's anything I can do for you. Goodbye."*

Call Back To Your Regular
Service & Repair People

Use this scenario to call and talk with people that you see on a regular basis who provide technical and repair services and help maintain your office and equipment. This would be a call between their regular visits — after you talked with them and made the request for help in person and they said to check back with them. You want their help in identifying people that they know that you can contact about working with you.

———

"Hi, <first name or nickname of your service provider>."

[Complete your small talk, and then get to the reason for your call.] *"When we spoke the last time you were here, I asked you who you might know or might have heard of in your travels who is in the market for a different home that should talk with me, and you told me that you needed some time to think of someone. I was wondering who you have thought of that I should contact?"* [Wait for response.]

[If he or she readily volunteers a name or two now, write it down and ask for a way to contact them. Be sure to note the correct spelling and pronunciation. Get first names so you don't sound like a telemarketer or solicitor, and get permission to use the person's name that is giving you the referrals when you contact the other people.]

They Have Names to Give You — *"That's great. I will call them and learn how I can help them. The next time you drop by I'll let you know what happened."*

"Can you think of anyone else?" [Wait for response.]

"Thanks. I appreciate your help. See you next time (or specific day if it's soon). Have a great day."

"By the way, have you passed out any of the business cards I gave you?" [Wait for response and discuss the circumstances if that if it has happened.]

"Thanks again. Goodbye."

No Names to Give You at This Time — *"That's quite all right. Thanks for trying."*

"Again, if anyone comes to mind that you think I should talk with, you can tell them about me, or you can let me know who they are whenever you come in and I'll contact them and see where it goes from there."

"I really appreciate your help. See you again next time. By the way, have you passed out any of the business cards I gave you?" [Wait for response and discuss the circumstances if that if it has happened.]

"Have a good one. Goodbye."

Call To A Professional

Use this scenario to call and talk with the professionals you know that are involved in your industry. This would be to people such as architects, stagers, loan processors, surveyors, home inspectors, and attorneys. You want their help in identifying people that they know that you can contact about buying or selling.

———

"Hi, <first name or nickname of your professional friend>."

[Complete your small talk, and then get to the reason for your call.] *"I think you know that I am selling real estate (I think you know that I opened my own real estate office/brokerage) in <name of general area or specific neighborhood or city>. I was wondering who might know or who you might be working with right now who has expressed an interest in selling their current home or moving and who hasn't selected a Realtor® yet that I should meet and talk with about how I might be able to help them."* [Wait for response.]

[If he or she readily volunteers a name or two now, write it down and ask for a way to contact them. Be sure to note the correct spelling and pronunciation. Get first names so you don't sound like a telemarketer or solicitor, and get permission to use the person's name that is giving you the referrals when you contact the other people.]

They Have Names to Give You — *"That's great. I will call them and learn how I can help them. The next time we talk I'll let you know what happened."*

"Can you think of anyone else?" [Wait for response.]

"Thanks. I appreciate your help. Have a great day. Goodbye."

No Names to Give You at This Time — *"That's quite all right. Thanks for trying. If anyone does come to mind that you think I should talk with about buying or selling, let me know who they are and I'll contact them to see how I can help them. I really appreciate your help.*

"Have a good one. Goodbye."

Call Back To A Professional

Use this scenario to call and talk with the professionals you know that are involved in your industry — after you've already spoken with them by phone or in-person — to learn if they have thought of any names to share with you. This would be to people such as architects, stagers, loan processors, surveyors, home inspectors, and attorneys. When you previously spoke with them, they said they needed some time to think of people, You are checking back now to see who they can tell you about for you to contact about buying or selling.

"Hi, <first name/ nickname of your professional friend>."

[Complete your small talk, and then get to the reason for your call.] *"The last time we spoke, you said that you needed some (a little) time to think of someone that you could share with me who is looking to move. I wanted to find out who you thought of that I should contact?"* [Wait for response.]

[Write down the name or names you are given, and ask for a way to contact them. Be sure to note the correct spelling and pronunciation. Get first names so you don't sound like a telemarketer or solicitor, and get permission to use the person's name that is giving you the referrals when you contact the other people.]

They Have Names to Give You — *"That's great. I will call them and see how I can help them. The next time we talk, I'll let you know what happened."*

"Can you think of anyone else?" [Wait for response.]

"Thanks. I appreciate your help. Have a great day. Goodbye."

No Names to Give You at This Time — *"That's OK. Thanks for trying. If anyone does comes to mind (If you think of anyone) that you think might be interested in moving, let me know who they are and I'll contact them to learn how I can help them."*

"I really appreciate your help. Have a good one. Goodbye."

Asking For A Referral On An Incoming Phone Inquiry

Use this scenario after talking with someone who called in from an ad or your website for information about homes you might have available — when you learn that they do not appear to like or want what you have to offer, that the home they called about has already been sold, or that they likely cannot afford to purchase anything that they might want or like — to ask for their help in identifying other people who might be interested in or capable of purchasing a new home.

———

"I appreciate your call and I am sorry that you don't think we can help you find a home suitable for you (you and your family), but let me ask you a question while I still have you on the phone (before you go)"

"Who can you think of who might be in a similar situation as you that you think might be interested in talking with me about listing their current home or searching for another one? I'd be happy to contact them and see if I can help them." [Wait for response.]

[If they volunteer a name or two, write it down and ask for a way to contact that person or persons. Be sure to note the correct spelling and pronunciation. Get first names so you don't sound like a telemarketer or solicitor, and get permission to use the person's name that is giving you the referrals when you contact the names they are giving you. Determine the best form of contact for the people who are being referred to you.]

They Have Names to Give You — *"That's great. Can you think of anyone else?"* [Wait for response.] *"Thanks for your help. I really appreciate it. Goodbye."*

No Names to Give You at This Time — *"That's quite all right. Thanks for trying and thanks for calling me. I appreciate your interest."*

"Let me know if I can help you in the future or if there are other properties you might want to see. Goodbye."

Post-Visit Call To Ask For A Referral

Use this scenario as a post-visit, post-meeting, or post-showing phone call to someone as part of a scheduled or planned contact or as a special call just to ask for their help in identifying other people who might be interested in working with you to sell their current home or look for another one.

"Hello <use their first name — even use their nickname if they indicated one when you met them>?"

"This is <your name> from <name of your company>. I really enjoyed getting to meet you (talking with you about our properties, showing you what is available for you to consider)."

"Now that you've had a chance to see some of the homes that are available for you to choose from (how I am marketing your home), maybe you've thought of some other people who ought to see for themselves what is available for them in the marketplace (who should see what I can do for them in listing their home). Who are the first two names that come to mind that I should call or email to let them know how I can help them?" [Wait for response.]

[Be prepared to write down any names they give you and ask for a way to contact those people. Be sure to note the correct spelling and pronunciation. Get first names so you don't sound like a telemarketer or solicitor. Get permission to use your resident's names when you contact the other people.]

They Have Names to Give You — *"That's great. I'll contact them and let you know what they said. Can you think of anyone else?"* [Wait for response.]

"Thanks for your help. I really appreciate it. Goodbye."

No Names to Give You at This Time — *"That's quite all right. Thanks for trying. Maybe the name of* *someone will come to you later that you can pass along to me."* [Set, confirm, or reiterate you next contact with them before concluding your call.]

"Again, thanks for your help (interest). Good-bye."

Call To Ask For Additional Referrals

Use this scenario as another reason to call someone after they already gave you the name or names of someone that you could contact — this time to thank them and pursue additional referrals.

———

"Hello <use their first name — even use their nickname if they indicated one when you met them>? This is <your name> from <name of your company>."

"When we met (spoke) the other day (a specific day), you gave me the name of <state the name or names of the people who were provided> as being in the market for a new home and possibly interested in letting me help them."

"I really appreciate you sharing their name (these names) with me, and I wanted to let you know that I called them and <report generally on your results>."

"I was wondering if you had been able to think of any other people who might be in the market for a new

home or who had expressed an interest in moving." [Wait for response.]

They Have More Names to Give You — *"Great. Who are they?"* [Wait for response.]

[Be prepared to write down any names they give you and ask for a way to contact those people. Be sure to note the correct spelling and pronunciation. Get first names so you don't sound like a telemarketer or solicitor. Get permission to use their name(s) when you contact the other people.]

"I'll contact these people just as I did the others that you gave to me and I will call you back to let you know what happens. Thanks again for your help. Goodbye."

No Names to Give You at This Time — *"That's quite all right. I appreciate your help."*

"By the way, I'd like to take you to breakfast next week (whenever our schedules allow within the next couple of weeks) to show my appreciation for your help." [Wait for response and agree upon a day, time, and location if they accept your invitation.]

"Would you like for me to call you or email you a reminder?" [Wait for response.]

Yes — *"Fine. I'll send you a note on <mention the*

specific day> to remind you of our appointment on <day, time, and location>. Which email address should I use?" [Confirm the address or write it down as you obtain it.]

"I look forward to seeing you then. Goodbye."

No — *"Fine. I'll plan on seeing you then on <mention the day and time> at <place>. Goodbye."*

Second Call To Ask For A Referral

Use this scenario to call someone that you talked with previously about referrals to ask them again for any names they can furnish. When you met or spoke with them previously they were unable to provide you with any names of people you could contact about potentially working with them to possibly list their current home or look at others homes.

————

"Hello <preferably use their first name — even use their nickname if they indicated one>? This is <your name> from <name of your company>."

"When we met (spoke) the other day (a specific day), I asked who you knew that might be interested in moving (looking for another home, putting their current home on the market, selling their present home), and you weren't able to think of anyone. "

"I thought that maybe since then that perhaps you'd thought of one or two people that I should contact to see how I can possibly help them."

"Who comes to mind (can you think of) now that you think I should talk to about what they have in mind as far as selling their present home or looking for another one?" [Wait for response.]

No Names to Give You at This Time — *"I understand, and I appreciate your time to talk with me again. Maybe later."*

"By the way, I'd like to send you our newsletter on a periodic basis just so you'll be aware of what's going on in the area in terms of real estate and community events. Is email OK?" [Wait for response. Confirm their email address or determine which one to use. You can also talk about or send them a link to your blog if you have one.]

"I'll check back with you in a few weeks to make sure you're getting the newsletter, and if anyone comes to mind that you think I should contact, you can tell me (let me know) then. Goodbye."

They Have Names to Give You — *"Great. Who are they?"* [Wait for response. Write down any names they give you and ask for a way to contact those people. Be sure to note the correct spelling and pronunciation.

Get first names so you don't sound like a telemarketer or solicitor. Get permission to use their name when you contact the other people.]

"I'll call them and discuss what they want to do and how I can help them. Then I'll call you after I have spoken with them to let you know what happened."

"Thanks for your help. I really appreciate it. Good-bye."

Leaving A Voice Message After A Brief Initial Meeting

Use this scenario when you get the person's voice mail when you call after meeting them at a business or social function. Be prepared to leave a voice mail message, but only leave the following message — and only do it on the initial call. After that, no messages regardless of how many times you call and reach the machine. Just hang up before the tone. For your friends, you can choose to leave a message or just call back.

———

"Hi, <their first name>. This is <your complete name, first and last> of <your company>."

"I met you briefly last night (the other day, Tuesday, last Wednesday, over the weekend) at (mention the

specific event or place where you met, such as Chamber of Commerce breakfast, church, jury duty, Little League game, the mall, a specific store or restaurant, the Rotary Club, PTA, etc.) — basically just long enough for us to exchange business cards." [Be sure to mention the place or the circumstances for the meeting.]

"I was calling to say hello again and see if we could set up a time to talk for a few minutes over coffee to learn more about each other's business. I possibly could use your help."

"I'm sorry I missed you. I'll try again another time, but my number here is <telephone number>."

"Thanks. I look forward to talking with you again soon."

[If they call back, that's great. Be prepared to have a conversation with them just as if you had reached them successfully when you telephoned originally. If they don't call back, call them again but do not leave any more messages.]

Leaving A Message With An Assistant

Use this scenario when someone other than the person you are calling answers the phone, or the person you are attempting to call is not available. Be prepared to leave a message with their assistant or whoever volunteers to take a message, but only leave the following message — and only do this on the initial call. It's not necessary that you leave a message, but if you choose to do so, be careful not to leave too many details because you don't want the assistant or the "screener" to try to help you or to tell you that the person who are calling (even if they are a friend) would not be interested in helping you.

———

[Begin this way when someone other than the person you are calling answers.] *"Hi, is <use their first name> in today (available)? This is <your name, first and last>."*

[Act like you are old friends even if you don't know them all that well — and only mention your company name if specifically requested.]

[If you decide to leave a message rather than just saying that you'll call back without providing any other information, you can go ahead with the following.] *"I met him (her) briefly last night (the other day, Tuesday, last Wednesday, over the weekend) at (mention the specific event or place where you met, such as Chamber of Commerce breakfast, church, Little League game, jury duty, the mall, a specific store or restaurant, the Rotary Club, PTA, etc.). I was calling to continue our conversation."*

"I'll try again another time. Thank you." [Don't volunteer your phone number. Provide it you choose to if you are asked for it, but it's not necessary. Just say that you'll call back later.]

[OR]

[For someone you know fairly well] *"He/she knows who I am, and I'll call back another time."*

[You may try calling again, but do not leave a second message — just your name.]

6

Reaching Out In Writing

The Value Of Writing

In addition to using personal and telephone communication with people that you already know, sometimes it might be easier or more convenient to reach out to them with a letter, email, or text message.

It isn't always quicker or as effective as talking to someone in person or by telephone, but you can do it according to your schedule and not be concerned whether the person you are connecting with is available at that particular moment to receive your message.

Using a written message, such as email, card, or letter — not text or instant messaging — is also useful for documenting your requests and for passing along your contact information.

When you need to include a postcard, your business card, or a survey, written communication is the best form of contact to use.

Letters work well also when it's been a long time since you have talked to your friend or customer. They help re-establish your relationship. Then you can follow with a phone call or email.

Using Email

While email is not appropriate for working with people that you don't know because it's less formal and their spam filter may not allow your message to get through, it's fine to use emails for communicating with friends and others that you know.

When you send emails, your email address and your company website address (URL) should be **active links** so that the person you're contacting can reply back or go to your website without entering any information.

They can just hit the link ("'control' + 'click'") and go right to a reply screen with your email address already filled in, or they can go directly to your website homepage.

Also, go for a consistent look in your email address. Don't use yourname@gmail.com address part of the time and yourname@yourcompany.com at other times.

Even though you are communicating with friends, do not use a personal-looking email address unless you are such good friends that they will easily recognize it.

Most of the time, addresses such as "fredlikesfishing@," "packersfan@," or "mary1267@" are too casual for business communication.

If you don't have an email at your community or corporate domain name — or choose not to use it since your friends may not recognize it — go with a gmail or yahoo email address.

Getting Email Delivered

You want the person who receives your email message to open it and read it, so avoid anything that might keep it from getting into their inbox.

If you're not sure how their email client accepts attachments, it's best not to include them and to put them in the body of your email. Keep them very short.

People worry about viruses, and some email programs could reject your message, or send it to the junk folder.

In your subject line, avoid anything cutesy or vague. Putting the name of your company or anything to do with real estate may get flagged. Just include your own name, such as *"Message from Steve Hoffacker."*

Familiarity Helps

Unlike contacting strangers where a certain amount of formality and propriety are important, connecting with your friends and people you know can be more casual and spontaneous.

Messages can be brief and can include more personal references. You can ask about them and their family or recall a common activity, for instance.

Don't be sloppy — you are still conducting business. However, phrases, some slang, and even humor can be used to help it sound more conversational with your friends. Avoid anything off-color.

Email is never advisable for an initial introduction to someone you are attempting to establish a relationship with but is fine to use with people you know. Just make sure you have a current email address before reaching out to them.

Texting And Instant Messaging

Text messaging ("texting") may be a good way to contact some of your closest friends and relatives — especially if you have texted them previously about others matters or know that they like to communicate this way. Perhaps they have texted you previously. It can be a good change of pace for contact.

Nevertheless, texting should never be done to introduce yourself to someone you have not met and should only be used when you know the person well enough for them to appreciate that you contacted them in this way and for them to respond to your text.

Even social networking sites like Facebook and Twitter can be great resources for leaving messages and communicating with your friends and network.

Using "chat" on Facebook or instant messaging on other sites — when you notice friends and acquaintances online — is an excellent way to initiate or maintain contact with them.

Writing Requires Minimal Effort

In this chapter, I've assembled just a few examples of letters, cards, and emails (and a couple of text messages) that you can use as you contact people that you do business with, those you have met socially or at business functions, ones you see occasionally, friends that you see often or rarely, people you have shown homes to or made sales with, professionals whose services you use, or others that you want to communicate with in writing about what you are doing and how you can use their help.

Remember the reason you use the letter, card, or email is to communicate when a personal approach is not practical or necessary. Having your message delivered must happen before it can be read.

Use these suggested letters, cards and emails exactly as they are or modify them for your writing style, personality, and degree of formality.

Intentionally, the suggested letters are a little more formal, printed cards a little so, and notecards fairly short and informal since they are handwritten. The suggested emails are in a relatively informal email style with more paragraphs that a letter.

Writing Is Only One Approach

Remember that the reason you are using the letter, card, email, or even in a few cases a text message, is to communicate to people you already know when you do not need to actually be speaking directly to them by phone or in-person — or when reaching them by phone or seeing them in-person is not easily done.

In some cases, this approach might be sufficient. In others, this will be a prelude to a phone conversation or meeting.

Your purpose in contacting people will vary also, from informational to a request for help.

They should not have a strong sales message.

Since people already know you, you don't have to convince them to read your message.

Your Signature Block

In the interest of keeping the following examples of letters as short as possible — showing just the salutation and main body of the letter — the following information (even if you already have mentioned it elsewhere in the body of the letter, such as your phone number, email address, or website) should be added after the text provided as a way of closing the letter:

Sincerely,
<space>
<Community or company name — or both >
<space>
<Your signature> (digital for emails)
<space>
<Your name — as people know you or you want to be called — plus any professional designations>
<Your position or title>
<Your direct phone line or extension>
<Your fax number>
<Your cell phone number>
<Your email address> (linked in emails)
<Your company website> (linked in emails)
<Your company blog address> (linked in emails)
<space>

<Your community or company "tagline">
<space>
<Your social media widgets> (linked in emails)
<space>
<Any attachments or enclosures>

Signing Cards

For notecards and postcards — especially ones that are handwritten or commercial greeting cards — just sign them in your own hand. Don't use a stamp or electronic signature

Using just your first name is fine — especially if you know them very well. For others that you know but aren't sure if they will recognize you by just your first name because they likely know several people with your same first name or you haven't talked with in a while, you might want to use your complete name.

You don't need to sign your name with your professional designations or title. That information, along with your pertinent contact information, will be on your business card that you are enclosing.

Put your business card in the envelope along with the note or place it inside the greeting card (obviously this can't be done with a postcard). Don't be concerned about some of your contact information being printed elsewhere on the card.

For emails, include hot (active) links to your email address, website, blog, social media profiles, and any references that you include.

The Inside Address

Unlike a letter to someone that you haven't met before, most of your letters to your circle of contacts will be less formal and therefore won't require an inside address.

When you are sending a letter to someone you just met as the first step in developing the relationship, you may want to use a customary inside address with:

> *<**Name**, including any professional designations>*
> *or <**Names**, if a couple>*
> *<**Title or Position**, if applicable>*
> *<**Name of Business**, if sent to the business>*
> *<**Business Address**, including department, suite number, floor, or building, if sent to the business>*
> *<**Home Address**, including apartment number, if sent to the residence>*
> *<**City, State, Zip**>*

For notes, cards, emails, and text messages — and for the majority or your letters — the inside address would not be used. However, it's a good idea to put the date at the top of any letter, card, or note that you are sending — even if there is no inside address.

Letter After A Brief Introduction

Use this letter — typically written on your computer and printed out although it can be handwritten if you like —after meeting someone briefly at a business or social function to acknowledge the meeting and set up a future telephone conversation with them. At that future meeting, you can enlist their help and pursue a business relationship with them. Keep this letter fairly brief and cordial — no sales message.

———

\<First name of new friend or acquaintance\>,

I'm glad I had the opportunity (chance) to meet you last night (Tuesday, yesterday, recently) at \<specific event or place where you met, such as seminar, mixer, reception, Chamber of Commerce breakfast, church, Little League game, youth soccer game, seminar, Rotary Club, etc.\>. Unfortunately, we didn't get a chance to talk to each other very much. It seemed like we just met long enough to exchange business cards and that was about it.

I would like to learn more about your business and get a chance, as well, to tell you about what we are doing here at \<name of your community or company\>. I will give you a call in a couple of days to see when you are available to grab a cup of coffee so we can talk some more.

In the meantime, you may reach me at <telephone number> or email me at <email address>. You might also want to visit our (my) website at <website address>.

I look forward to talking with you again.

Printed Notecard After
A Brief Introduction

Rather than a letter (handwritten or printed), you may choose to use a notecard, such a one imprinted with the name and logo of your company that you can print out with your message on your computer. Use this after meeting someone briefly at a business or social function to acknowledge the meeting and set up a future telephone conversation. At that future meeting, you can enlist their help and pursue a business relationship with them. Notes are typically brief and to the point — avoid a sales message or reference.

<First name of new friend or acquaintance>,

I'm glad I had the opportunity (chance) to meet you last night (Tuesday, yesterday, last week) at <specific event or place where you met, such as seminar, mixer, reception, charity event, golf outing, Home Builders Association or Realtor® Association event, Chamber of Commerce breakfast, church, Little League game,

youth soccer game, Rotary Club, committee meeting, etc.>.

I will give you a call in a couple of days to see when you are available for coffee so we can talk some more.

In the meantime, you may reach me at <telephone number> or email me at <email address>.

You might also want to visit our (my) website at <website address>.

I look forward to talking with you again.

Handwritten Notecard After
A Brief Introduction

You may want to use a handwritten note on your company notecards rather than a computer printed message to contact someone you just met at a business or social function to set up a future telephone conversation. Just write as legibly as you can. You may want to print in all caps if your penmanship is not strong. At that future meeting, you can enlist their help and pursue a business relationship with them. You want your note to be cordial and fairly brief.

———

<First name of new friend or acquaintance>,

I'm glad we met last night (Tuesday, yesterday, last week) at <specific event or place where you met, such as seminar, mixer, reception, charity event, golf outing, Home Builders Association or Realtor® Association event, Chamber of Commerce breakfast, church, Little League game, youth soccer game, Rotary Club, committee meeting, etc.>.

I will give you a call in a couple of days to see when you are available for coffee so we can talk some more.

In the meantime, you may reach me at <telephone number> or email me at <email address>.

You might also want to visit our (my) website at <website address>.

I look forward to talking with you again.

Handwritten Note In A Greeting Card After A Brief Introduction

You can choose to use a handwritten message inside a commercial greeting card (a card with a success message or one with an inspirational picture and message) rather than using a note or letter — just jot your message in the blank space above the fold or on the left side of the fold of the card to contact someone you just met at a business or social function to set up a future telephone conversation. At that future meeting, you can enlist their help and pursue a business relationship with them. You want your note to be cordial and very brief.

―――――

<First name of new friend or acquaintance>,

I'm glad we met last night (Tuesday, yesterday, last week) at <specific event or place where you met, such as seminar, mixer, reception, charity event, golf outing, Home Builders Association or Realtor® Association event, Chamber breakfast, church, Little League game, youth soccer game, Rotary Club, committee meeting, etc.>.

I will give you a call in a couple of days to see when you are available for coffee so we can talk some more.

I enclosed my card with my contact information.

I look forward to talking with you again.

Email After A Brief Introduction

Email is a very acceptable and convenient way for businesspeople and friends to communicate today, so you may choose to use this rather than a letter, note, or card to contact someone you just met at a business or social function to set up a future telephone conversation. At that future meeting, you can enlist their help and pursue a business relationship with them. This is a fairly informal method of contact and should be used within 24 hours of the original meeting.

<First name of new friend or acquaintance>,

I'm glad I had the opportunity (chance) to meet you (I enjoyed meeting you) last night (this morning, yesterday, over the weekend, Wednesday morning, Monday night) at <specific event or place where you met, such as seminar, mixer, reception, Chamber of Commerce breakfast, church, Little League game, youth soccer game, the mall, a specific store or restaurant, Rotary Club, etc.>.

I would like to learn more about your business and what you do. Also, I might be able to use your help.

I'll give you a call in a couple of days to see when you are available to get (have, let me buy you) a cup of coffee.

If you like, you can contact me at <telephone number> or <email address> [linked].

You might also want to check out (take a look at, visit) our (my) website at <website address> [linked].

I look forward to talking with (seeing) you again.

Letter To Friend Or Acquaintance

Use this letter on your company letterhead to notify friends and acquaintances of your new position and to lay the foundation for referrals. This is going to be a more casual and informal style of letter than most you would use. Keep it relatively short since you can visit with them later or use text, phone, or email to pursue your referral needs. Keep this letter strictly informational, as you don't want to appear that the only reason you are contacting them is for their help.

————

\<First name of your friend or acquaintance\>,

I don't know if you've heard or not, but I wanted to make sure you knew (are aware) that I am now representing \<your company\>.

I just wanted to make sure you were aware of what I'm doing and that you have my current contact information.

I'll call you soon to see (discuss, talk about) when we can get together (have coffee, get a drink, grab lunch, have breakfast).

In the meantime, feel free to call me anytime on my cell phone at \<number\> or email me at \<email address\>.

Printed Notecard To A
Friend Or Acquaintance

Rather than a letter, you may choose to use an informal note or notecard card imprinted with the name and logo of your company that you print out on your computer to notify friends and acquaintances of your new position and to lay the foundation for referrals. The note format is good because you want to keep it relatively short anyway since you can visit with them later or text, phone, or email them to pursue your referral needs. Keep this note strictly informational — you don't want it to appear that you are contacting them strictly for their help.

——————

<First name of your friend or acquaintance>,

I wanted to make sure you are aware (know) that I just started representing <name of your company. (I've changed companies since we last spoke, and now I'm here at/with <name of your company>.)

I'll call you soon to give you some more details and see when we can get together for a cup of coffee (breakfast, lunch).

For now, I just wanted to make sure you were aware of what I'm doing and that you have my current contact information. Feel free to call me anytime on my cell phone at <number> or email me at <email address>.

Handwritten Notecard To
A Friend Or Acquaintance

Use this personal handwritten notecard on your official company notepaper or notecard to notify your friends and acquaintances of your current status and to lay the foundation for referrals. Keep this note strictly informational, as you don't want it to appear that you are contacting them just for their help. You may want to print in all caps rather than use cursive.

————

<First name of your friend or acquaintance>,

I wanted to make sure that you're aware that I just started representing <name of your company>. I've just been here <approximate length of time>.

I'll call you soon to give you some more details and see when we can get together for a cup of coffee (breakfast, lunch, a drink).

I just wanted to make sure you were aware of what I'm doing and that you have my current contact information.

Email To A Friend Or Acquaintance On Your New Position

Email is a convenient way to communicate with friends and acquaintances as long as you have their current email address. This informal message is a great way to let people know what you are doing and to lay the foundation for referrals. This note should remain primarily informational, but there can be some personal references in it because of the format. Just don't make it seem that you are contacting them just for their help.

_____

<First name of your friend or acquaintance>,

Just a quick note to let you know that I've relocated (moved) from my last position. I wasn't sure if you knew about this so I wanted to make sure I told you that I recently started selling real estate here at <name of your company>, located at <physical address or landmark>.

I've attached a vCard with my new contact information, and I'll call you soon to see (discuss/talk about) when we can get together.

In the meantime, feel free to give me a call on my cell at <cell number> or email me at <email address> [linked].

Talk to you soon.

Email To A Friend Or Acquaintance For A Referral

After you have re-established contact with your circle of contacts, email is a great way to reach out to some of them to request the names of people for you to contact that might be interested in moving.

_____

<First name of your friend or acquaintance>,

When we last spoke (talked) I told you about my current real estate sales business with <name of your company>, and I mentioned that I could use your help in identifying people that might be looking to buy or sell.

Has anyone come to mind that I could talk to? Just let me know who I should be talking to, and then let them know that I will contacting them.

Thanks for your help.

Text Message To A Friend, Relative, Or Acquaintance For Update

Use this brief text message to contact someone you know well enough to communicate with them in this way (relative, close friend, or acquaintance) to let them know of your new position and to set up another contact by phone — or have an email or text mail exchange with them. For purposes of this template, abbreviations that often are used in texting will not be used. However, if you have already been texting this person and typically type all in lower case or use shorthand or abbreviations, then using "4" for "for," "cn u" for "can you," "ur" for "your," "BTW" for "by the way" and other such notations or styling would be fine to use. Otherwise, avoid them and keep it businesslike.

<Their first name>, I just started selling real estate here at <name of your company> in <general location>. Would love to catch up with you over coffee. What's your schedule (convenient for you)? <Your first name>

Text Message To A Friend, Relative, Or Acquaintance For Referral

Use this brief text message to contact someone you know well enough to communicate with them in this way (relative, friend, or acquaintance). You want to find out who they know that might have an interest in moving that they can refer to you. Again, if you have already been texting this person and typically use shorthand notations, it's fine to continue doing that. Otherwise, keep it businesslike.

<Their first name>, I can use your help. I think I told you that I am selling real estate in <name of your area> with <name of your company>. I would appreciate hearing about anyone that you know who might be interested in moving. Any ideas? Thanks. <Your first name>

Email To A Social Networking Contact

Use this email message to contact any person that you know through social networking sites that you have blogged with or connected with online. You mainly want

to talk with them by phone or have an email exchange —
rather than set a meeting — to determine who they know
who has an interest in moving that they can refer to you.

_____

<Their first name>,

*[If you're contacting them through the social
networking site and using the email platform there,
there won't be a need for establishing how you know
each other. Otherwise, an opening line reminding
them of how you know each other might be necessary.]*

*As you probably know, I sell real estate in <name of
your area or town> with <name of your company>.*

*I thought maybe you could help me. I am looking for
people who might be interested in moving within or
relocating to my area — now or in the near future.*

*If you have any ideas, I would appreciate hearing
about them. If you can't think of anyone, that's OK.
Maybe later.*

Thanks for your help.

Email To A Realtor® Friend

Email is a convenient way to reach out to Realtors®
that you know to let them know about your new

position and to request referrals. Because you both are interested in possibly making a sale at your community, you can go ahead and ask for a referral on the initial contact with your friend.

––––––

<First name of your Realtor® friend or acquaintance>,

Just a quick note to let you know that I've changed offices (relocated), and I'm now with <name of your company>, located at <physical address or landmark>. I wanted to make sure that you knew about this change.

I'll give you a call soon to talk more about each other's listings and how we might be able to help each other.

I've attached a vCard with my new contact information.

Talk to you soon.

Letter To A New Purchaser

Use this letter that you generate on your computer to contact someone who has purchased a home from you regardless of whether they have actually moved into it yet. Your letter thanks them for doing business with you and requests their help in identifying people that you should talk with about what you offer.

––––––

<First name or names of your new purchaser>,

I appreciate your trust and confidence in letting me help you find your new home.

As you are getting ready to move into (getting settled in) your new home, you probably have had several friends ask about your new home and show an interest in what you have selected.

I would love to talk with (show) anyone that is looking for a new home what is available for them.

I have enclosed a stamped, addressed postcard for you to jot down the names and contact information for a couple of people that have said they would like to live in a different home or sell their present one. If you prefer, you can email it to me at <email address>.

Thanks for your help. If there's anything I can do for you, please let me know. It won't be much longer until you're ready to move in.

Printed Notecard To A New Purchaser

Rather than a letter, you may choose to use a notecard imprinted with the name and logo of your company that you print out on your computer to contact a new purchaser. It's less formal than a letter. This note is used to thank them for doing business with you and ask for referrals.

———

<First name or names of your new purchaser>,

I appreciate your trust and confidence in letting me help you find your new home.

As you are getting ready to move into your new home, you probably have had several friends ask about your new home and show an interest in what you have selected.

I would love to talk with (show) anyone that is looking for a new home what is available for them.

I have enclosed a stamped, addressed postcard for you to jot down the names and contact information for a couple of people that have said they would like to live in a different home or sell their present one. If you prefer, you can email it to me at <email address>.

Thanks for your help. If there's anything I can do for you as you are getting ready to move-in, please let me know.

Handwritten Notecard
To A New Purchaser

Instead of mailing something "typed," you may want to use something much less formal such as a handwritten notecard imprinted with your company name or logo and basic contact information on it to thank your new purchaser and ask for a referral.

———

<First name or names of your new purchaser>,

I appreciate your trust and confidence in letting me help you find your new home. I could use your help in identifying some of your friends that you think might like to find a new home also.

I have enclosed a stamped, addressed postcard so you can let me know about anyone that you think I should talk to. If you prefer, you can email the information to me at <email address>.

Thanks for your help. If there's anything I can do for you, please let me know.

Handwritten Greeting Card
Note To A New Resident

Rather than anything "typed," or even a handwritten notecard, you may choose to use a commercial greeting card with a "Congratulations" or "Thank You" cover and inside message. Keep the note short and on the blank space opposite the printed message. Use this to thank a new purchaser and to request referrals.

———

<First name of new purchaser>,

Thanks again for allowing me to work with you to select your new home.

As you are getting settled in your new home, I'd really appreciate it if you could let me know about anyone that might be thinking of moving also. Be thinking of who that might be and then you can let me know the next time we talk.

Thanks for your help. If there's anything I can do for you, please let me know.

Email To A New Purchaser

Email is a convenient way to reach out to a new purchaser to thank them for doing business with you and ask for a referral.

———

<First name of your new purchaser>,

I appreciate your trust and confidence in letting me help you find your new home, and I have enjoyed getting to know you. I could use your help in identifying some of your friends that might like to find a new home also.

I would love to talk (meet) with them and show them (talk about) what is available to meet their needs.

Just hit the "reply" button above and send me the names and contact information for a couple of people that they would like to find another home (are interested in moving).

Thanks for your help. If there's anything I can do for you as you getting ready to move-in, please let me know.

Letter To An Exiting Customer

Use this typed or computer printed letter to contact someone who has purchased from you in the past. Make sure they are still in the home you sold them before sending out this letter. Your letter should again thank them for doing business with you and request their help in identifying people who might be wanting to move.

_____

<First name or names of your customer>,

I appreciate being able to work with you when you bought your current home, and I could use your help in identifying others who might be looking for a home.

I would love to be able to talk with some of your friends who have expressed an interest in selling their current home or finding another one.

Please use the enclosed stamped, addressed postcard to jot down the names and contact information for anyone that you think I should talk with — or you can email it to me if you prefer at <email address>.

Thanks again for your help. Let me know if I can do anything for you.

Printed Notecard To An
Exiting Customer

Rather than a letter, you may choose to use a notecard imprinted with the name and logo of your company that you print out on your computer to contact someone who has purchased a home with you in the past. Make sure they still occupy that home. It's less formal than a letter, and it is nice way to ask for referrals.

———

<First name or names of your customer>,

I appreciate being able to work with you when you bought your current home, and I could use your help in identifying others who might be looking for a home.

I have enclosed a stamped, addressed postcard for you to jot down the names and contact information for anyone that you think I should talk with — or you can email it to me if you prefer at <email address>.

Thanks again for your help. Let me know if I can do anything for you.

Handwritten Notecard To An Exiting Customer

Instead of mailing something "typed," you may want to use an informal handwritten notecard to reach out to your existing customers and ask them for referrals. Just make sure that they still live in the home you sold them.

———

<First name or names of your customer>,

I appreciate being able to work with you when you bought your current home, and I could use your help in identifying others who might be thinking of a move.

Please jot down the names and contact information for anyone that you think I should talk with on the enclosed postcard or email it to me if you prefer at <email address>.

Thanks again for your help. Let me know if I can do anything for you.

Email To An Exiting Customer

Use this less formal email message for a more immediate way to reach out to your existing customers and ask for referrals. Make sure they still live in the home you sold them.

<First name or names of your customer>,

I appreciate being able to work with you when you bought your current home, and I could use your help.

I would love to be able to talk (meet) with some of your friends that might be thinking of selling their current home or getting another one.

Just hit the "reply" button and send along (include, furnish) the name, email address, and phone number for anyone that you think I should contact.

Thanks again for your help. Let me know if I can do anything for you.

Letter After An Open House

Use this typed or computer printed letter to contact someone who visited your open house (provided you obtain their mailing address when you meet them) to thank them for attending and cultivate the relationship that you began at the open house, regardless of how much time you spent talking with them. You want to meet with them to discuss their needs in more detail, and you are interested in referrals even if they decide not to move — or if they were just curious neighbors. If it is a couple, address the letter to both of them.

––––––

<First name or names of your open house visitors>,

Thanks for visiting the open house at <street address> today (this afternoon, yesterday). I appreciate you stopping by to take a look.

As you could tell we were quite busy [if this was the case], and I didn't get to spend as much time with everyone as I would have liked. Still, I'm glad I got the opportunity to meet and talk with you (the two of you).

I would like to explore your needs in a little more detail, so I'll be calling you to set up a time when we can do that and possibly look at some homes.

If your needs are more distant rather than immediate, perhaps you can think of people that might be interested in looking for a different home or in putting theirs on the market.

Again, thanks for visiting.

Handwritten Notecard After An Open House

Instead of mailing something "typed," you may want to use something less formal such as a handwritten note on your company's letterhead or notecard stock to thank people for attending your open house and ask for referrals.

<First name or names of your open house visitors>,

Thanks for visiting the open house at <street address> today (this afternoon, yesterday).

I appreciate you stopping by to take a look and would like to find out a little bit more about what you're looking to do.

I'll be calling you to set up a time when we can talk some more. In the meantime, perhaps you can think of other people that might be interested in looking for a different home or in putting theirs on the market.

Again, thanks for visiting.

Email After An Open House

Instead of mailing something — typed or handwritten — use this informal email message for a more immediate way to contact people who visited your open house as you thank them and ask for referrals. You must obtain their email address at the open house in order to use this. Mail it within 24 hours and preferably the day of the open house.

———

<First name or names of your open house visitors>,

Thanks for visiting the open house at <street address> today (this afternoon, yesterday). I appreciate you stopping by to take a look.

As you could tell we were quite busy [if this was the case], and I didn't get to spend as much time with everyone as I would have liked. Still, I'm glad I got the opportunity to meet and talk with you (the two of you).

I would like to explore your needs in a little more detail, so I'll be calling you to set up a time when we can do that and possibly look at some homes.

If your needs are more distant rather than immediate, perhaps you can think of people that might be interested in looking for a different home or in putting theirs on the market.

Again, thanks for visiting.

7

Making It Work

An Entrepreneurial Approach

As a Realtor® responsible for your own production and income, you are an entrepreneur. No customers are guaranteed or provided (except those who respond to your marketing and arrive on their own).

Some may come through advertising and marketing, but they don't come in a box you can purchase at the office supply store.

Each day, you essentially start from scratch. You don't know how many you'll have a chance to talk with or who they will be. Some days there might not be anyone who walks through your front door or otherwise contacts you.

You examine your options for customers — the lifeblood of your business — and determine that you have three viable choices.

Your Three Customer Options

Option one — you stay in your office and take floor time to meet people who call or walk in — or you take phone calls or emails you from traditional marketing sources that you or your company pay for and utilize.

This includes all forms of print advertising in newspapers and magazines (including real estate guides), electronic media (such as radio and TV), internet (your website, social media, and internet advertising), and referral traffic from other brokers.

Of course, you maintain post-visit Follow-Through® contact with everyone who contacts you according to their level of interest and ability to make a decision on listing their current home or selecting one that you are showing them.

Option two — you reach out to people you don't know or haven't met. You involve strangers in your business and begin building sales and referrals with their help.

This is discussed in my companion book for lead generation: *"Expanding Your Sphere: Connecting With Strangers For More Realty Listings & Sales."*

Option three — you talk to people you already know and begin developing your own leads with them. That is what we have been discussing in this book.

It's these second and third options that are going to give you the additional edge and earning power over other Realtors® and real estate salespeople in your market.

Most of them are content to work with the traffic that walks through their front door or that which is created through incidental broker contacts and referrals.

This is unpredictable and short-sided. It is not a dependable or consistent form of lead generation.

Empowering Yourself For Success

With the knowledge that you can produce your own leads and make traffic and new business appear that you have generated, you can be an outstanding success.

This is powerful.

Some leads you will generate from people that you haven't met yet. You'll focus on making new connections with strangers and learning which ones you might be able to help and which can lead you to their friends.

However, starting with your circle of contacts and beginning there is very empowering. There is no pressure to meet people before you can start asking for help. Begin with people that you think might be looking for a new home themselves or can introduce you to others.

As long as you don't give the impression that your friendship is conditioned upon them working with you or giving you a referral, your friends will still be your friends whether they can help you or not.

Knowledge is power, and in this case it is knowing that you can produce the traffic and sales leads you need to be successful. This is in addition to what your broker or office provides through conventional or traditional marketing and advertising — or in place of it.

Begin acting as if the only traffic you're going to get is what you produce for yourself. Then anything your broker or company supplies is a bonus.

Empowerment Is Taken

By generating your own leads — by reaching out to people that you don't know as well as utilizing your circle of contacts — you're going to be adding an element to your sales program that most Realtors® and real estate salespeople are missing.

There is no effective limit to the number of leads that you can generate this way.

This truly can make the difference in your success and enable you to thrive in your marketplace when other Realtors® and brokers are just competing for the same pool of people to list their homes or buy others.

Empowering yourself to begin generating your own leads — by working with friends or strangers — is not something you have to be invited to do or given permission to start.

Empowerment is taken. It is not given.

Just decide that generating your own leads is something that makes sense for you to do — even if you're not totally comfortable with the idea of approaching your family, friends, and acquaintances and talking with them about your real estate sales business.

However, just doing that will empower you to begin expanding your business and taking responsibility for producing the most crucial element of your sales program — your future customers.

Going Beyond The Obvious

While talking to people that you already know and asking them for referrals will net you many additional opportunities to make sales, other aggressive brokers and Realtor® can do the same thing.

They may not be as comprehensive as you are or able to identify the variety of people you can contact, but starting with referrals from existing satisfied customers and from family and friends are common ways to generate more business.

Add to that, the referral network that most Realtors®️ and brokers try to attract for selling their listings, and you'll soon see that this is quite competitive.

However, when you begin to contact more than just your friends and Realtors®️ from other offices that you know — more than just the obvious — you'll be doing what hardly anyone else in your market is doing.

When you reach out to people that you know professionally, ones that you know through the construction industry, merchants that you patronize, and even "lost sales," you're going to be finding opportunities that just aren't there for the people who aren't looking for them.

Then, you can also use some of the scenarios that are in my companion lead generation book, *"Expanding Your Sphere: Connecting With Strangers For More Realty Listings & Sales,"* for meeting and working with strangers.

Reaching out to total strangers and strategically contacting other businesspeople and professionals in your marketplace that can help you in your business are ways that you can be intentional about expanding your business.

Few other brokers, Realtors®️, and real estate salespeople in your market will come close to the type of lead generation you'll be capable of producing.

Intentionally Going After Success

Making the decision that you want to have more business than you're getting now through traditional sources — and that you want it on a more consistent basis — is the first step to becoming a great sales lead generator.

It is a conscious decision, and it requires willpower. No one reaches this intentional decision without the earnest desire to act on it — unless it is just wishful thinking.

Wanting more business, like it sure would be nice to have, is entirely different than doing something to actually make it happen.

This works in all market conditions — very competitive markets to very stubborn ones.

As long as there are homes to sell and people to buy them, the techniques and strategies of traffic and lead generation that I've discussed will work for you.

You're In Charge Now

The amount of new business you can produce is limited only by your ambition and the amount of time devoted to it.

You have been given several scenarios in this book. Expand from there.

This is a good start, but it is not intended as a comprehensive list.

You have to own your customer base — not in a legal sense but in a responsibility one. You have to continually add to it so it doesn't get stale. Own the creation of additional leads.

Your paradigm needs to be that you're in charge of producing the people that you talk with about listing their current home or purchasing another one.

Act as if the only people you're going to get to talk with are what you produce for yourself.

Then anything else that comes your way through traditional marketing or incidental referrals is a bonus.

Not every person you talk to — even though you know them — will want to or be able to help you, but as long as you are committed to developing your own leads, you are going to be successful.

You hold the key.

Steve Hoffacker

Steve Hoffacker, AICP, CAASH, CAPS, CGP, CGP, CMP, CSP, MCSP, MIRM, is principal of Hoffacker Associates LLC, a West Palm Beach, Florida based real estate and new home sales training company, marketing consultancy, and commercial real estate brokerage.

Steve is an award-winning new home sales trainer, real estate sales coach, marketing consultant, award-winning photographer, commercial real estate broker, blogger, and best-selling author of instructional sales books.

For more than 30 years, he has helped homebuilders, new home salespeople, contractors, Realtors® and real estate sales professionals, small business owners, and entrepreneurs to be more visible, competitive, profitable, and effective — and to really enjoy what they are doing.

One of the keys to increased production and profitability is Steve's innovative customer connection program of intentional lead generation, customer rating, social networking, and post-visit contact that lets you reach out to potential customers, attract new leads, identify those people who are ready to make a decision, and maintain appropriate contact with others who need more time.

As a result, you will be making sales that otherwise might not have happened, and you can eliminate unnecessary expenditures of time, money, and energy in the process.

www.ingramcontent.com/pod-product-compliance
Lightning Source LLC
Chambersburg PA
CBHW061316220326
41599CB00026B/4899